MONSTER
STOCK LESSONS

2020–2021

By
John Boik

ISBN: 979-8-4126-5963-3 (paperback)

This text contains trademarks, service marks, or registered trademarks of ©StockMaster. Investor's Business Daily and IBD are trademarks of Investor's Business Daily, LLC.

This publication is designed to provide accurate and authoritative information in regard to the subject matter covered. It is sold with the understanding that the author is not engaged in rendering legal, accounting, futures/securities trading, or other professional investment advice services. This publication is for educational and research purposes only.

Contents

Introduction

Monster Stock Lessons will walk you through the years of 2020 and 2021 in the stock market and analyze many of the leading stocks that reached monster stock status. Just to clarify, that was defined in *Monster Stocks* as follows:

A stock that at least doubles in price in a short time frame. A short time frame in the stock market, as far as history with monster stocks is concerned, usually lasts between 4 and 18 months. Most will land somewhere in the middle of that range as the meatiest part of a fast-advancing monster stock usually occurs between 6 and 12 months of its major move. And many of the truly giant monster stocks will triple, quadruple, or even move up a thousand percent or more in those short time frames.

The year 2020 produced many strong leading stocks after Q1, which had produced a steep bear market (defined as a decline of 20% or more from its recent highs) in one of the shortest periods of time in stock market history. But coming off that quick bear market was a handful of market leaders that drove the market higher through the remainder of 2020 and into 2021. That is why you should never give up on the market when it corrects—you will miss out on some of the best opportunities when the market turns up. For those who did give up near the end of Q1 in 2020, they certainly missed out on some great opportunities when dozens of stocks reached top-notch status in a short period of time. But many of the biggest leaders that became monster winners in 2020 didn't continue leading in 2021, even though the market kept its uptrend intact. You will see why it is critical to adhere to selling rules when they present themselves. You don't want to give back most of the profits you attained on the way up. We will analyze how and why that occurred so the lessons learned can be remembered in future market cycles. But while some leaders gave up their leading stock status from the prior year, there were others that thrived in 2021, during a somewhat choppy uptrend. We will see how the market generated new leaders as sector rotation was more commonplace in 2021 than in 2020.

Studying history in the market helps us understand how cyclical trends work and how new opportunities occur while also giving clues as to how leading stocks top and begin downtrends. And continuing uptrends always produce new leaders that take off and lead. One thing to note when analyzing these two years—the monster stock status, measuring a stock that's doubled or more in one year, will be looked at on a calendar basis. I'm only doing it that way so you can see some leaders that doubled in a calendar year and how many times those opportunities arose. Of course, many leading stocks will double over time frames that cross over yearly calendar dates. But seeing it on the yearly calendar basis gives one a look into how many leaders are produced that way and how they provided big gains. And it only takes a few monster stocks a year, if handled correctly, to produce index beating returns, as you will soon see. You will never get the full move of a monster stock, and you never get them all. Your objective should be to recognize which stocks show the characteristics of past winners and trade them within their uptrend moves to garner a portion of the profits they offer on their incredible runs.

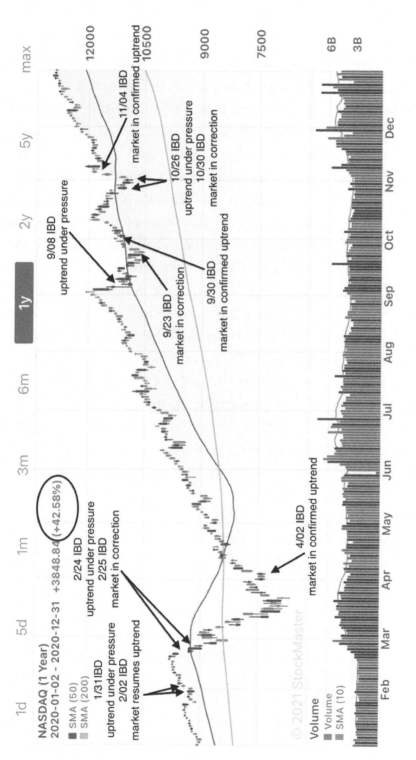

Figure I-1 Nasdaq Daily Chart 2020. (StockMaster)

In analyzing the years of 2020 and 2021, I will provide you with several guideposts used to gauge the action of the market in general and the leading stocks. The main source of information I've used is *Investor's Business Daily* (*IBD*). Their decades of experience in analyzing the markets health day-to-day is invaluable. Figure I-1 shows the Nasdaq chart where *IBD* made market interpretation change calls during 2020 as the health of the market changed (confirmed uptrend, uptrend under pressure, market in correction, and uptrend resumes). These calls occur as the market changes and most stocks typically will follow the market. There were three instances in 2020 where *IBD* classified the market as "market in correction." The first was near the end of February when heavy selling was starting to hit the market due to COVID-19 concerns. That was the start of the sharp but short bear market. There were two others—one at the end of September and one near the end of October. Both of those pullbacks in the market were short lived, and soon the market regained its upward momentum. The strong uninterrupted uptrend from April through August was where most of the best stock gains occurred. The last two months of the year were also very strong for leading stocks.

New Highs / New Lows

One of the other guideposts I use to check the overall health of the market is the net differential between 52-week new highs and new lows. There are many secondary market indicators out there, maybe too many. Some are good, some not so much. After years of research, the one I found that provides a guidepost to the market averages with consistent reliability is the ratio of 52-week new highs to new lows. I call the differential between the two the High Low Gauge or H/L/G. I track it every day and compare it to what the overall market averages are doing. It's important to point out that this is still a secondary indicator. Nothing beats daily observations of the price and overall volume action in the main market indexes along with the stocks that are leading an advance or coming under selling pressure during a decline. But the H/L/G has a solid history of matching or leading market action. If you think about it, it makes sense. You can't have a strong uptrending market without more stocks making new highs than those making new lows and vice versa. And there are different stages and degrees of market uptrends and downtrends. Some may be stronger or weaker than others. Some are choppy and much more difficult to maneuver through. Many times, the level or trend of positive and/or negative days or weeks in a row of the H/L/G helps determine the level of health of the overall market. There certainly are trends to it and levels of excessiveness and weakness within it have matched up to the action of the market with surprising accuracy. I won't go into all the details of those in this book. Dr. Alexander Elder's book (see below) describes many of those levels.

I'm not the first person to see this correlation by any means. The ratio has been around for decades and is used by many stock research firms regularly. Gilbert Haller wrote a book in 1965 called *The Haller Theory of Stock Market Trends*. His extensive study of the markets focused on the importance of the ratio of new highs to new lows. He states that he "quickly charted a NH-NL Index covering several years, and found that it was indeed an important factor in measuring technical market strength or weakness." Figure I-2 is from his book. He calculated his ratio on a weekly basis. The year 1960 was mostly a down year for the market, with several large whipsawing trends in the middle of that year. You can see how his NH-NL Index correlated with that trend. The year 1961 produced a very strong uptrend through most of May and then the market corrected hard starting in late May, which lasted through late July. A strong bounce then led to choppy trading until December when another strong correction hit the market. You can clearly see in figure I-2 how his index of weekly net new highs and new lows correlated directly with the actions of the market during those two years, as just one example. He also followed the number of stocks that advanced and declined on a weekly basis and calculated what he called his Advance and Decline Index.

Dr. Alexander Elder, an author of many excellent market books, wrote one of his books dedicated to the study called *The New High – New Low Index* (that I highly recommend). A few key points from that book include his discovery of how the index can be a leading indicator of the stock market by days or weeks. His research shows that certain timing of buying, selling, or doing nothing with stocks, can improve by following the trend and level of the index. Also, based on the level and activity of the index, one can gauge how strong or weak a trend in the market is likely to continue in either direction. You will see how accurate this has been during the two years covered in this book.

Gerald Loeb, who in my opinion was one of most successful traders ever for over five decades, covering the 1920s through the 1970s, used the ratio regularly as well. Many top traders today track the ratio daily and compare it to the action of the overall market. I use the daily new high and new low numbers that *IBD* produces on its subscriber website. They take out stocks selling for under ten dollars per share and stocks that trade under ten-thousand shares per day. The *IBD* numbers, therefore, take out the insignificant stocks in the market. The *IBD* numbers will then vary from other sources that include all stocks traded. The tracking of this has been remarkably accurate in relationship to the health of the general market,

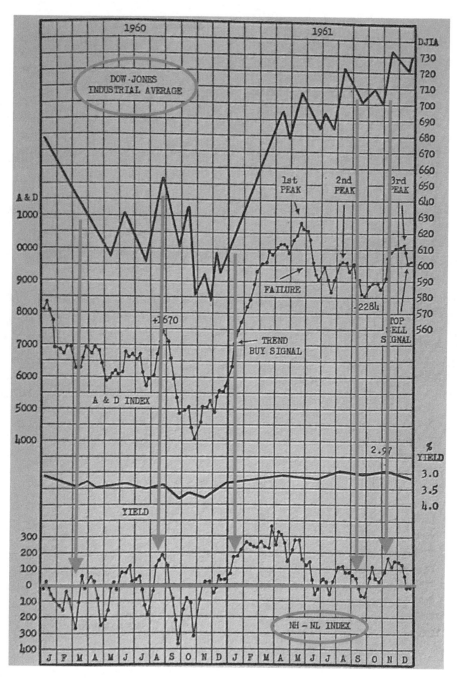

Figure I-2 NH-NL Index to Dow Jones Index 1960–1961.

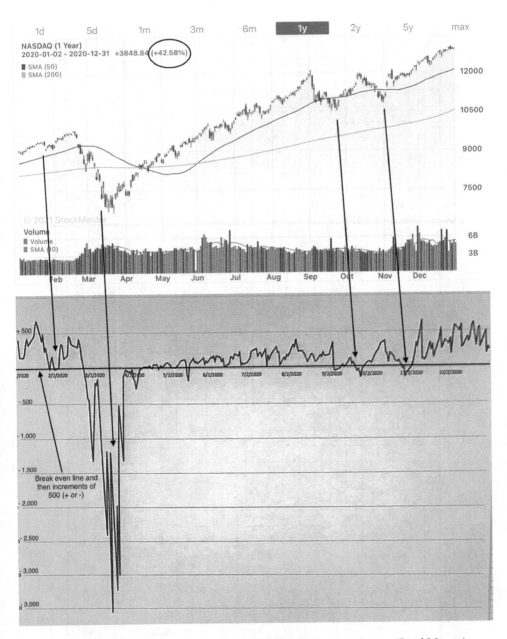

Figure I-3 Nasdaq Index 2020 and Net New Highs to New Lows. (StockMaster)

just as Haller discovered back in the 1960s. Figure I-3 is a chart of the Nasdaq for 2020 and under that is a chart of the net New High/ New Low gauge differential that I calculated daily from the *IBD* site. One can clearly see the correlation between the two. (The chart below, due to its framing correlating to the market, doesn't line up perfectly, which is why I draw the arrows from one to the other, connecting the same time frames.) In Chapter Two, I show the same information for 2021.

MVP Stocks

When tracking leading stocks that become monster stocks, there are certain traits that nearly all historic big winners shared. Keeping it simple helps as well. This short book won't go into the fundamental statistics for each stock analyzed. Suffice it to say that all monster stocks throughout history had strong fundamentals during their upward moves. If they didn't possess the earnings or sales growth power at the prior or immediate time, it was anticipated that strong earnings growth and solid sales growth were soon to become significant factors in the stocks' continued rise. If the numbers disappointed during the run, that would often mark the end of a stock's uptrend. And since many of the stocks analyzed here come from *IBD* lists, you can be assured that the fundamentals play a big role behind or ahead of a stock's performance.

Many top traders run screens to sort through hundreds of stocks, looking for setups in bases, support areas, climax runs, and so on. Relative Strength (RS) is a great measure of the strength of a stock as it relates to all other stocks and is a favorite measure to track for many successful traders. I use *IBD* for my screening tool, as they perform a highly selective criteria for stocks to make the several lists they produce weekly, and they update them daily, based on current price action. *IBD* has strict criteria for a stock's fundamentals and relative strength, so you can be assured that the stocks they list are leaders from a current or perceived earnings and sales standpoint and from a price performance standpoint.

When doing research for *Monster Stocks*, which came out in 2007, and being active in the market, I found that simple critical criteria have remained the same over the years and over different market cycles. That is not surprising given the market hasn't changed much over history due to human nature being the main factor. The key technical criteria I discovered that was common to all were moving averages, volume, and price action. When stocks possess action that relate positively to all three, I call them MVP (moving average, volume, price) stocks. Just as in sports or business, your MVPs are the standout performers. It's the same in the stock market. MVP stocks tend to become monster stocks. And monster stocks are the top leading stocks in all market uptrends.

Moving Averages

A highly successful, legendary trader once stated, "Nothing good happens below the 200-day moving average line." That area is used as a bottoming area for many future leading stocks after a major correction and is looked at as a long-term average. Many leading stocks will find support there and start base building. But growth stocks that move up to monster status left that area behind some time ago. As they rise up, they cross over the 50-day area as they construct healthier basing patterns. The 50-day area is viewed as a more intermediate-term moving average. William J. O'Neil and many institutional as well as individual traders, have used this area as a metric in measuring a stock's overall strength or weakness. Rising 50-day moving average lines indicate a stock is in an uptrend. The

21-day area (basically one month of trading activity) is a shorter intermediate-term moving average and has become more accepted over the years and is used by many top traders. It was mentioned several times in *Monster Stocks* and illustrated its importance during a monster stocks performance run. The shorter-term metric is the 10-day moving average and is also used by many top traders. I use a simple system for grading my stocks, which is similar to school grading. This helps me categorize stocks in a very easy manner. I like to own only A and B graded stocks.

A – above the 10/21/50/200-day moving averages
B – above the 21/50/200-day moving averages but below the 10-day moving average
C – above the 50/200-day moving averages but below the 10/21-day moving averages
D – above the 200-day average but below the 10/21/50-day moving averages
E – below all the moving average areas listed above

For purposes of this short book, I will show the 21-day and 50-day simple moving averages on the charts featured. As I stated, the 200-day area on these charts had already been crossed and was in the rearview mirror for leading stocks at this stage in their set up, breakout, and run up. I'll mention the 10-day moving average from time to time, but most of the action, breakout, run up, and top will focus on the 21-day and 50-day moving average areas. Those are your short to intermediate time frames that typically produce the most monster stocks and the meatiest part of their strong moves upward. The strongest stocks of all will ride and be above all the moving averages mentioned.

Volume

Volume has been and continues to be a critical measurement of the demand for a strong rising stock, and its correlation with price action is the most definitive signal of how strong or weak a stock has been and could potentially be. Volume activity has been a critical tracking component for many of the best stock traders throughout history and many of the top traders today. Volume is also a characteristic of liquidity, based on its average daily trading volume. For purposes of this book, I analyze and feature only stocks that traded, on average, one million shares or more per day. Those are typically stocks that institutional investors favor. And if they want to be involved in a stock, they leave footprints (in volume levels) behind that are hard to hide. It is their involvement in a stock that accounts for the major moves. And as an individual trader, it should be your objective to find where the big money is placing its commitments and follow it.

The charts in this book will consistently point out volume action and how it played a key role in a stock's price movement. Whether it's green (positive volume action on strong up days) or red (negative volume action on strong down days), volume is a key determinant of a stock's trend. Your objective is to be on the same side of the trend in a leading stocks move. Remember, the trend is your friend, and you don't fight against your friends.

Price

Price is the definitive measure that we all want on our side. Everything concerning a stock (fundamentals, news, opinions, etc.) ends up reflected in its price. Either to the upside or the downside, as a trader you are managing your risk level by the changes in price, and those changes determine your decisions to buy, sell, hold, or avoid a stock altogether. It's your risk management techniques, the proper timing of the price changes based on the markets activity, and the leading stocks in your trading that will determine how successful your results will be. We all want to maximize our profits, and one way to do that is to invest and trade in the leading stocks that perform the best and become monster stocks.

The Charts

The stock analysis charts included will point out key price action characteristics of each stock. The main technical signals highlighted will be breakouts from basing areas, volume signatures (both on the upside and downside), and how the stock acted near the key 21-day and 50-day areas. Notice I use the word areas many times instead of lines. Stocks that find support at those key areas rarely just come down perfectly to touch those lines and bounce right off of them (though you will see a few here). Many great stocks undercut moving average lines and can stay under them for several days or more without doing much damage. Volume levels should be watched closely during those times as they can give off vital clues if the stock recovers or continues to falter near those key areas.

Most of the gap-ups (and gap-downs) on the charts that you will see are the result of earnings announcement reactions. Buying into gap-ups is a strategy of many top traders. Many traders trim positions before an earnings announcement due to the high-risk levels associated with disappointing reports and the hard-negative reactions or gap-downs that can result from disappointments. Solid earnings reports that exceed expectations can many times lead to after hours and opening gap-ups that show institutions piling into the stock with strong volume buying power.

With stocks that double and become monster stocks during their run, you will typically find pullbacks soon after. Pullbacks occur many times on the way up during a leading stocks run as they get extended in price and traders take some profits. Many top traders sell portions of their position in a leading stock into strength when stocks power up quickly. Implementing sell strategies on the way up and buying strategies near key support areas will be addressed in Lessons Learned.

I would encourage readers to study *Monster Stocks* to get more in-depth descriptions of many of the concepts presented here. This book is also intended to be a chart study book. It focuses on the best of the best performers for the years featured. Studying the best MVP performers can help one in future market cycles as patterns do repeat in the market. Please make sure you view all the charts and study and understand the key points in each—chart study is one of the best teachers of the market. Many of the best stock traders throughout history became master chart readers. Price and volume analyses are key—they have been throughout history, and they proved it again in 2020 and 2021, both on the way up and on the way down. How stocks behave around key moving average areas can also give vital clues as to what big money investors and traders are doing. Do those areas become support or resistance for a stock? Are they trending up or down? These are all key components in an uncertain environment like the stock market. All the charts featured here come from the app ©StockMaster. I use that app daily, and I highly recommend it based on its ease of use and its many features.

Chapter One – 2020

The new decade started off with a bang as the market continued, following up on the strong Q4 uptrend from 2019. Chinese stocks were some of the leaders at the time, including BABA, TIGR, EH, and MOMO (I will use ticker symbols when referring to stocks most of the time in this book). Other leaders were LITE and PYPL, just to name a few. January was positive, but near the end of the month, we start to hear about and get a glimpse of the early impacts from COVID-19.

By the third week of February, COVID-19 was starting to have a major impact. A string of distribution days occurred in the markets, the first trend of negative net New High / New Lows (H/L/G) since the beginning of Q4 in 2019 set in, and leading stocks were breaking down through key moving averages on volume signatures. As the month progressed so did the selling. Heavier selling was hitting the markets by the last week of February. *IBD* changed their market outlook status to "uptrend under pressure" on February 24 (see figure I-1). The next day *IBD* changed their outlook again, this time to "market in correction" as heavy selling continued. March was a panic sell month as the indexes tanked and COVID-19 concerns started to make a big impact. As William J. O'Neil once stated, "When they raid the house, they usually get everyone, and eventually all the leaders will succumb to the selling." That certainly seemed to be the case as the month of March 2020 will go down as one of the worst in market history.

With the fear of COVID-19 spreading and its possible impact on everything from health care, work habits, sports and entertainment to travel, social gatherings, and so on, the market reflected it all in its downward spiral. After four straight weeks of heavy selling through the third week of March, the Dow Index was already down 33% YTD (See figure 1-1).

However, a few stocks bucked the heavier selling and began to show some signs of life. With companies closing offices and a work-from-home environment starting to take hold, some stocks that represented a new look for work started to quickly halt the selling pressure and show promise. That is why one should never give up or take their eyes off the market. Even during the harsh selling

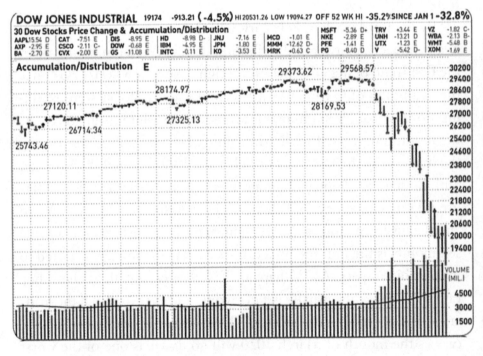

Figure 1-1 Dow Jones Index Chart Jan 2020 – March 2020. *(IBD)*

downtrends that stocks will cycle through, it's wise to pay attention as an uptrend can always be right around the corner. And stocks that hold up best during a downtrend will typically become the monster stocks of an ensuing uptrend. It's happened throughout market history and it was no different in the spring of 2020. Here are a few from the weekend of March 21, 2020 (figure 1-2). Here's something to note: when I include figures of watchlists from my *IBD* research that show annotations, those are from my personal trading journal at the time.

Zoom (ZM) and DocuSign (DOCU) were seen as early stocks that would benefit a work force that was forced to work remotely. Zoom had already been rising throughout the four-week market route while DocuSign fell hard initially but recovered quickly on huge volume. GSX pulled back to its 50-day area during the selling but found support at that time.

Selling began to slow the last week of March, and the H/L/G, which I calculate from *IBD*, while still negative, was now in the low two-digit figures (see figure I-3) as opposed to numbers in the thousands seen just weeks before. Excessive levels of constant negative readings in the thousands rarely last longer that a few weeks

Figure 1-2 Weekend Chart Watchlist – March 2020. (*IBD*)

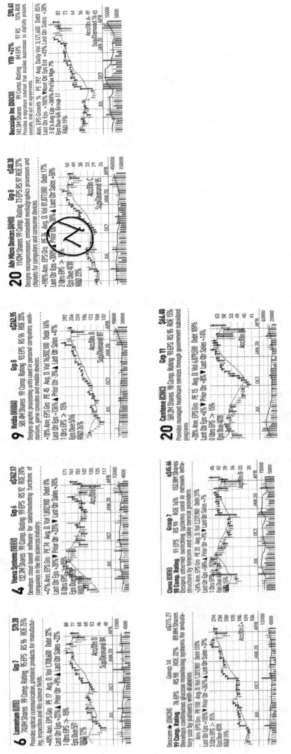

Figure 1-3 Weekend Chart Watchlist – April 2020. (*IBD*)

based on market history. That relates somewhat to the forecasting ability this gauge can show at times. In the past, readings of excessiveness, both on the positive and the negative side, often led to changes in market direction. On April 2, 2020, *IBD* changed their market outlook to "market in confirmed uptrend" (see figure I-1). More stocks started to rise, and some potential leaders were showing positive volume action and key moving average support. On April 9, 2020 the H/L/G turned positive for the first time since February 21, breaking a negative 33-day trading streak. Figure 1-3 is a list of some stocks showing potential during the second week of April.

After such a dramatic drop in the market over a short time frame, when an uptrend begins, there will be some rough days ahead, as all confirmed uptrends don't succeed. Many times the market will turn

Main Watchlist Watchlists ▽ - By Symbol ↑			
AMD	54.99	+0.06	0.11%
DOCU	100.53	+2.10	2.13%
JD	44.60	+0.74	1.69%
NFLX	426.75	+13.20	3.19%
VEEV	174.68	+1.09	0.63%
ZS	69.96	+3.48	5.23%
DOW J	23504.30	-445.50	-1.86%
S&P 500	2783.36	-62.70	-2.20%
NASDAQ	8393.18	-122.56	-1.44%

Figure 1-4 Market Watchlist – April 15, 2020. (StockMaster)

back to the downside and the new uptrend quickly fails. One way to see if an uptrend fails is to see if the first stocks that come out turn and quickly fail. One day that may have stood out during this time was April 15, 2020. On that day, the indexes fell hard again, but some of the stocks showing early promise bucked the selling. Figure 1-4 is an example from that day.

By the third and fourth week of April, with the market doing better, the recent uptrend continued on without failing. The world was changing in response to the impact of COVID-19. Here's a summary at that time from *IBD* of how the market was adjusting and the stocks that were getting attention from big investors.

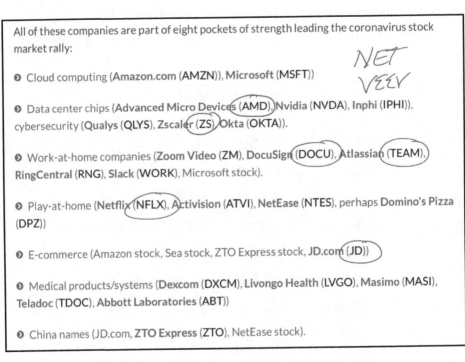

All of these companies are part of eight pockets of strength leading the coronavirus stock market rally:

NET
VEEV

❯ Cloud computing (**Amazon.com (AMZN)**), **Microsoft (MSFT)**)

❯ Data center chips (**Advanced Micro Devices (AMD)**, **Nvidia (NVDA)**, **Inphi (IPHI)**), cybersecurity (**Qualys (QLYS)**, **Zscaler (ZS)**, **Okta (OKTA)**).

❯ Work-at-home companies (**Zoom Video (ZM)**, **DocuSign (DOCU)**, **Atlassian (TEAM)**, **RingCentral (RNG)**, **Slack (WORK)**, Microsoft stock).

❯ Play-at-home (**Netflix (NFLX)**, **Activision (ATVI)**, **NetEase (NTES)**, perhaps **Domino's Pizza (DPZ)**)

❯ E-commerce (Amazon stock, Sea stock, ZTO Express stock, **JD.com (JD)**)

❯ Medical products/systems (**Dexcom (DXCM)**, **Livongo Health (LVGO)**, **Masimo (MASI)**, Teladoc (**TDOC**), Abbott Laboratories (**ABT**))

❯ China names (JD.com, **ZTO Express (ZTO)**, NetEase stock).

Figure 1-5 Market Commentary – April, 2020. (*IBD*)

From figure I-1, you can see the strong uptrend from April through August. That uptrend is where the bulk of the new leaders emerged and many reached monster stock status in that short time frame. The following charts will feature many of the liquid stocks that led that uptrend. Each chart will point out classic breakouts, pullbacks to key support areas, volume signatures, gap-ups, and activity at or near the key moving average lines of the 21-day and 50-day areas. As everyone tried to manage and adjust to COVID-19, there were changes taking place in the economic environment that produced new opportunities for lifestyles and companies. Some of the first stocks out of the gate were seen as benefiting from a new work-from-home environment. Among those already mentioned were Zoom Video (ZM) and DocuSign (DOCU). Both stocks were featured in *IBD*'s weekly chart lists at the time, did very well, and offered up several opportunities along the way to score nice gains.

Also benefiting from the work-from-home sector as early leaders were Peloton Interactive (PTON) and Etsy, Inc. (ETSY), among others. Several sectors that were also responding well in early April were data security firms and e-commerce technology firms. Leaders from the data security group included Cloudflare, Inc. (NET) and CrowdStrike Holdings (CRWD). Some Chinese e-commerce stocks continued to lead as well. Several of them were leaders during the latter part of 2019 and into the first few months of 2020. Some of those leaders who came up again and broke out with the new uptrend included Pinduoduo, Inc. (PDD) and JD.com, Inc. (JD). As the uptrend was broadening out and showed little signs of failing, more stocks stepped up as institutions put more money to work after the intense selling that occurred in March.

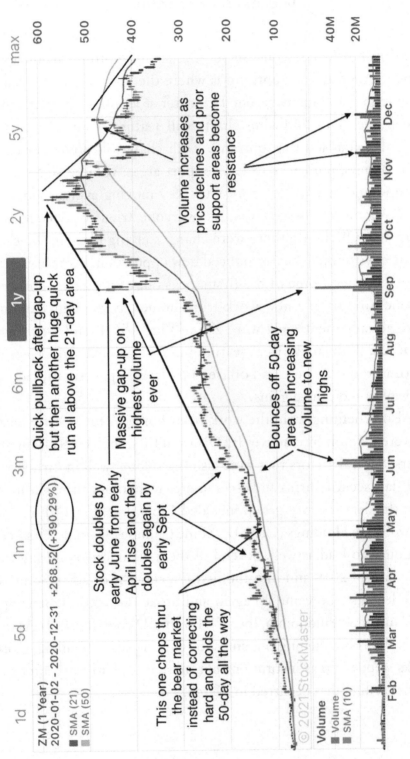

Figure 1-6 Zoom Video Comm. 2020 Daily Chart. (StockMaster)

The following text labels appear within the figure:

ZM (1 Year)
2020-01-02 - 2020-12-31 +268.52 (+390.29%)
SMA (21)
SMA (50)

Quick pullback after gap-up but then another huge quick run all above the 21-day area

Massive gap-up on highest volume ever

Stock doubles by early June from early April rise and then doubles again by early Sept

Volume increases as price declines and prior support areas become resistance

This one chops thru the bear market instead of correcting hard and holds the 50-day all the way

Bounces off 50-day area on increasing volume to new highs

© 2021 StockMaster

Volume
Volume
SMA (10)

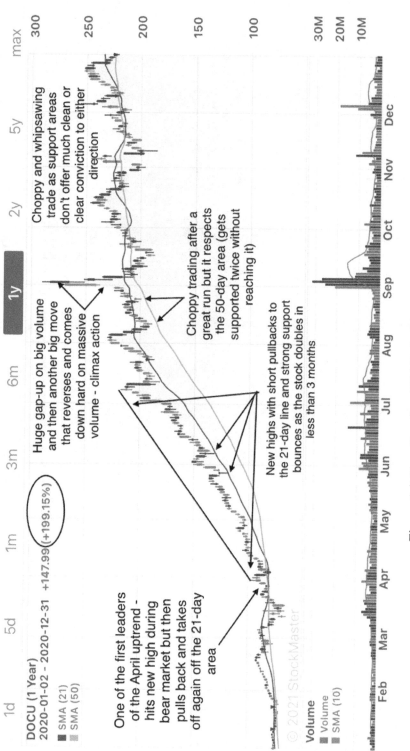

Figure 1-7 DocuSign, Inc. 2020 Daily Chart. (StockMaster)

DOCU (1 Year)
2020-01-02 - 2020-12-31 +147.99 (+199.15%)

SMA (21)
SMA (50)

Huge gap-up on big volume and then another big move that reverses and comes down hard on massive volume - climax action

Choppy and whipsawing trade as support areas don't offer much clean or clear conviction to either direction

Choppy trading after a great run but it respects the 50-day area (gets supported twice without reaching it)

One of the first leaders of the April uptrend - hits new high during bear market but then pulls back and takes off again off the 21-day area

New highs with short pullbacks to the 21-day line and strong support bounces as the stock doubles in less than 3 months

© 2021 StockMaster

Volume
Volume
SMA (10)

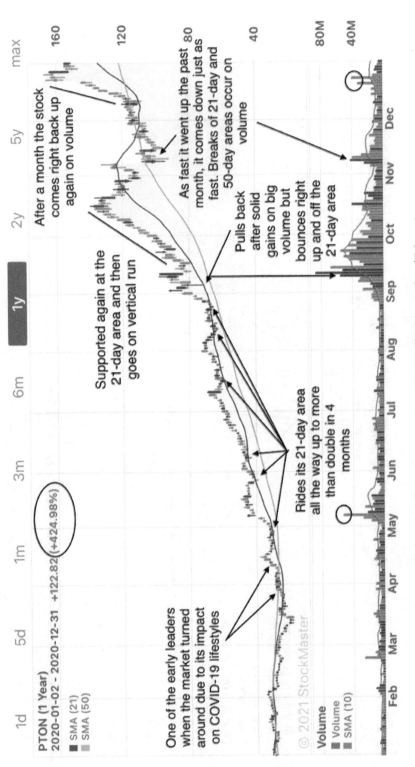

Figure 1-8 Peloton Interactive. 2020 Daily Chart. (StockMaster)

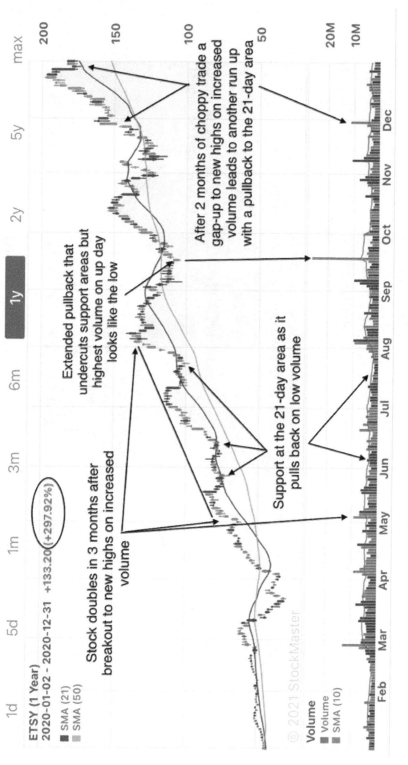

Figure 1-9 Etsy, Inc. 2020 Daily Chart. (StockMaster)

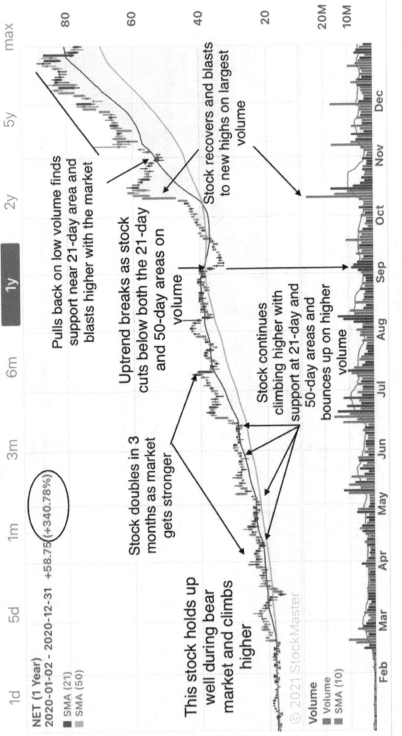

Figure 1-10 Cloudflare, Inc. 2020 Daily Chart. (StockMaster)

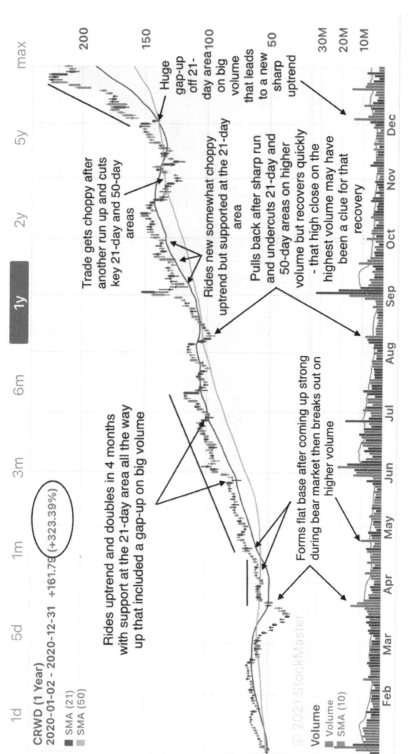

Figure 1-11 Crowdstrike Holdings. 2020 Daily Chart. (StockMaster)

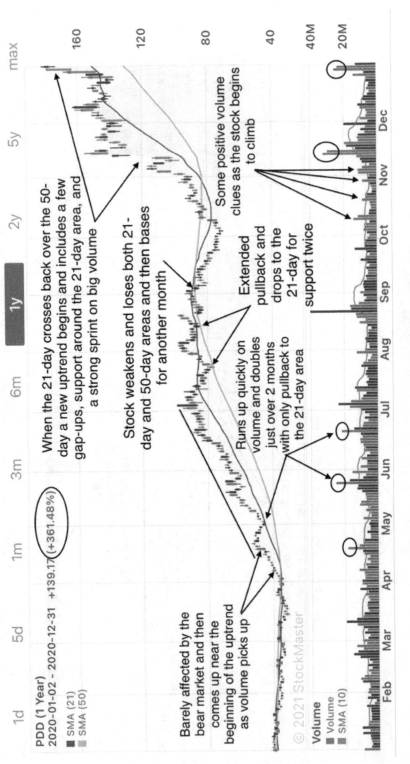

Figure 1-12 Pinduoduo, Inc. 2020 Daily Chart. (StockMaster)

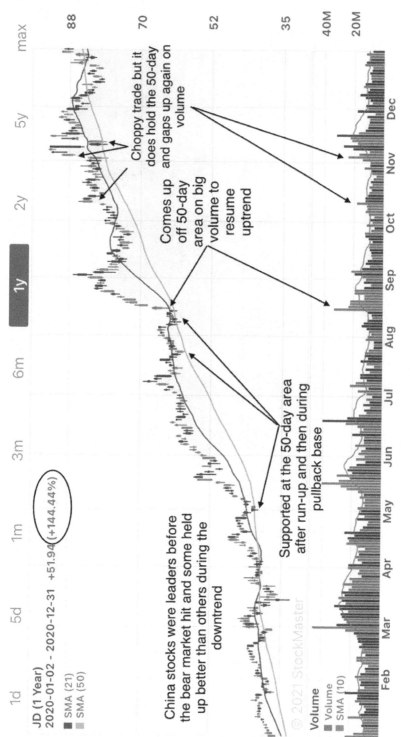

Figure 1-13 JD.com, Inc. 2020 Daily Chart. (StockMaster)

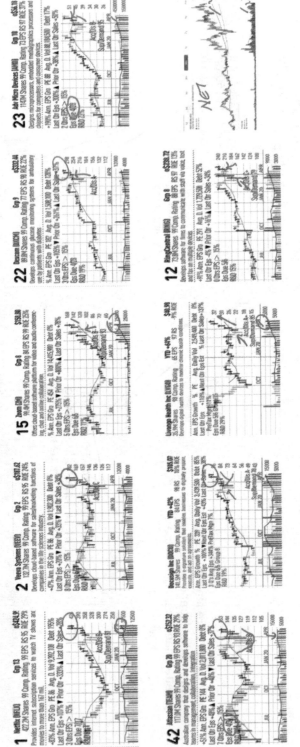

Figure 1-14 Weekend Chart Watchlist – April 26, 2020. (*IBD*)

Those charts show how early leaders begin to assert themselves when an uptrend starts and then builds momentum. A few struggled a bit in April but found support at key areas and then resumed their runs. By the end of April, more stocks were stepping up or building healthy basing patterns. As the uptrend attracted more investors, the buying power increased. Many times, the first ones out of the gate make the greatest gains and become the true market leaders that become monster stocks. You can see on the charts how most of them scored triple-digit gains during the year, including a few that showed topping signals before the year ended. As the year progressed, more stocks stepped up and some fell off the leader list. But that occurs during every uptrend in the market. To show what was happening as it occurred, I will show some watchlists throughout the year so you can see what stocks may have been setting up at that time.

Figure 1-14 is a watchlist from that late April time frame with some annotations pointing out some positive technical traits.

Included in that list was a solid leader Livongo Health (LVGO). The stock continued climbing, and near the beginning of August 2020, the company announced that it was being purchased in a merger transaction. The price had soared to over $140 per share after an incredible run in four months of over 400% (see figure 1-16). You will soon see how a few top traders made big gains on that stock. This list again included ZM and DOCU, as you can see them gaining leadership.

During May more stocks perked up and broke out or lifted up off key support areas in strong volume and became leading stocks. Datadog, Inc. (DDOG), Shopify, Inc. (SHOP), Twilio, Inc. (TWLO), PayPal (PYPL), Fastly, Inc. (FSLY), Draftkings, Inc. (DKNG), and

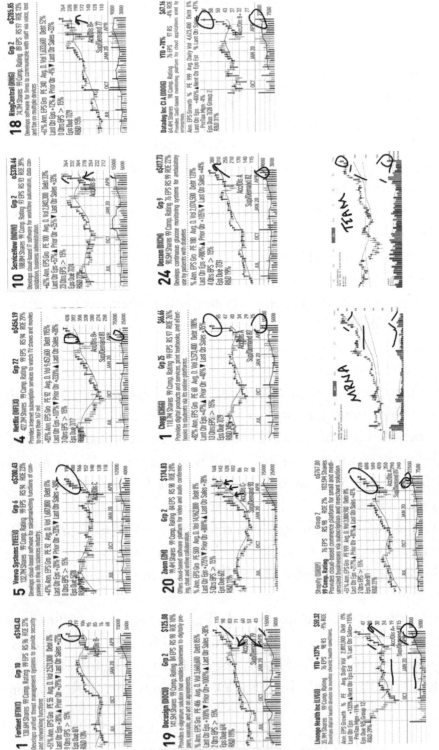

Figure 1-15 Weekend Chart Watchlist – May 15, 2020. (*IBD*)

Futu Holdings (FUTU) were some stocks making strong moves that led them to reach monster stock status over the remainder of the year. Some doubled up in very short order. The stocks made up a variety of technology and growth sectors that included cloud-based commerce and technology, digital payments, and online sports entertainment, as well as an additional Chinese leader.

Figure 1-15 is a weekly watchlist from May 15, 2020. You can see a few of the names just mentioned after they started their runs. There were many others that also scored nice gains. Top traders were now in many of these names, and they viewed this uptrend with more conviction as it went on without pulling back hard. Note that the watchlists are weekly charts (from my *eIBD* subscription), and the featured charts are daily charts (from the StockMaster app). William J. O'Neil and many other legendary traders started with weekly charts to begin their analysis and research. They all mentioned that weekly charts give a better indication of the bigger picture. If they noticed something forming on a weekly chart, they would then check the daily chart. They used daily charts more for detailed timing indications for trading. The use of both is needed, but weekly charts alert traders first on what to pay attention to, and daily charts are used to dig in a bit deeper. Many top traders today employ that same strategy. It's not that one is better than the other; they are used in conjunction with each other.

The market uptrend continued during the summer months with the major indexes experiencing only minor pullbacks. Many of the leading stocks already featured continued their runs. A few pulled back after some quick, strong gains. Some then built new bases while others found support at key areas and then bounced right back up to continue higher. There were plenty of new stocks joining in too.

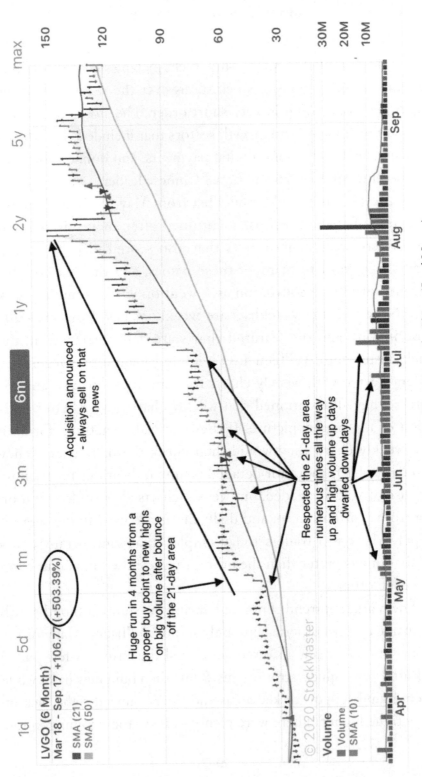

Figure 1-16 Livongo Health. 2020 Daily Chart. (StockMaster)

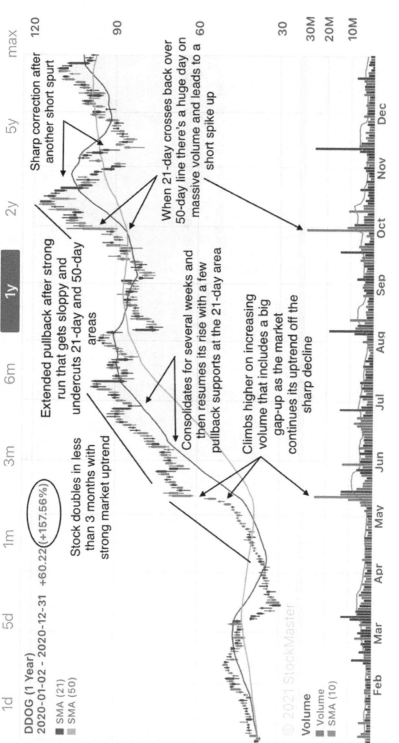

Figure 1-17 Datadog, Inc. 2020 Daily Chart. (StockMaster)

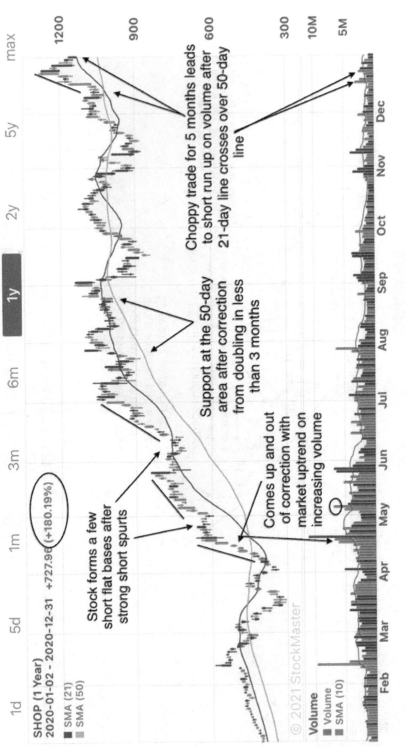

Figure 1-18 Shopify, Inc. 2020 Daily Chart. (StockMaster)

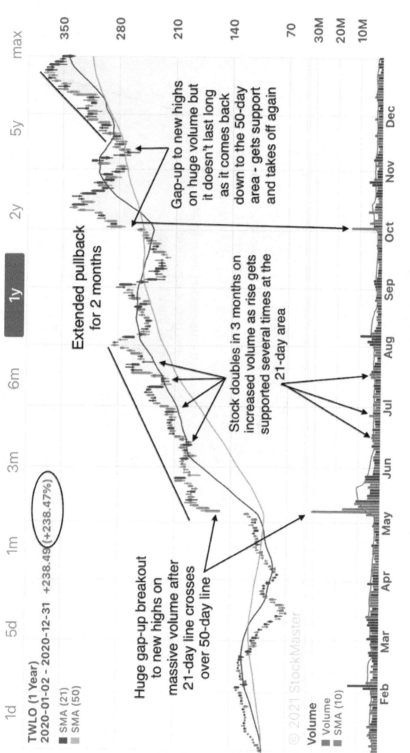

Figure 1-19 Twilio, Inc. 2020 Daily Chart. (StockMaster)

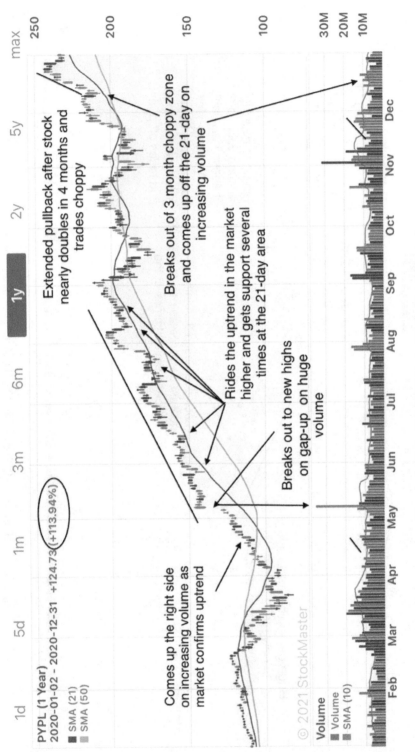

Figure 1-20 PayPal. 2020 Daily Chart. (StockMaster)

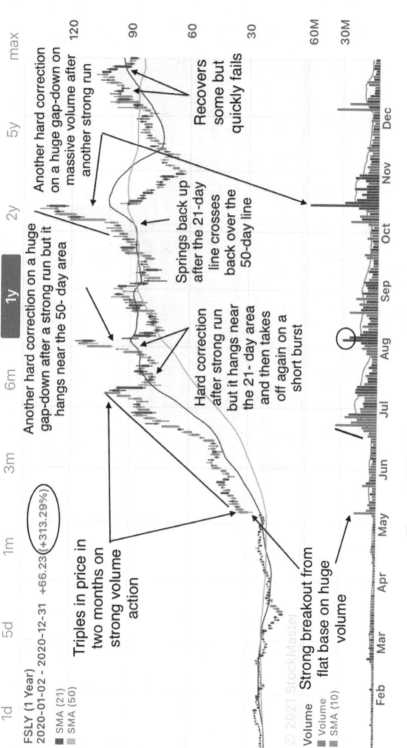

Figure 1-21 Fastly, Inc. 2020 Daily Chart. (StockMaster)

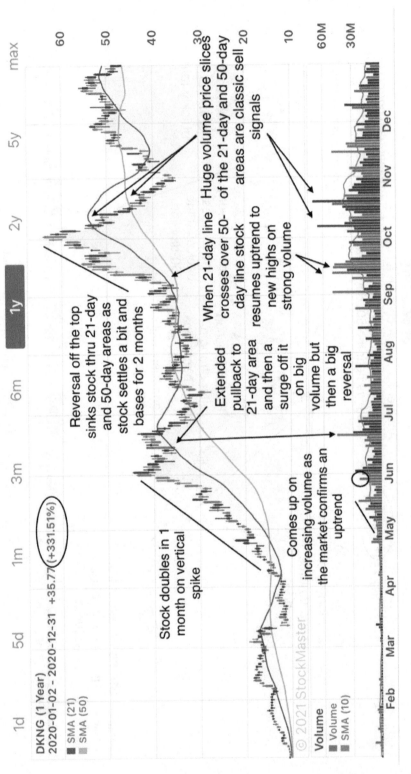

Figure 1-22 Draftkings, Inc. 2020 Daily Chart. (StockMaster)

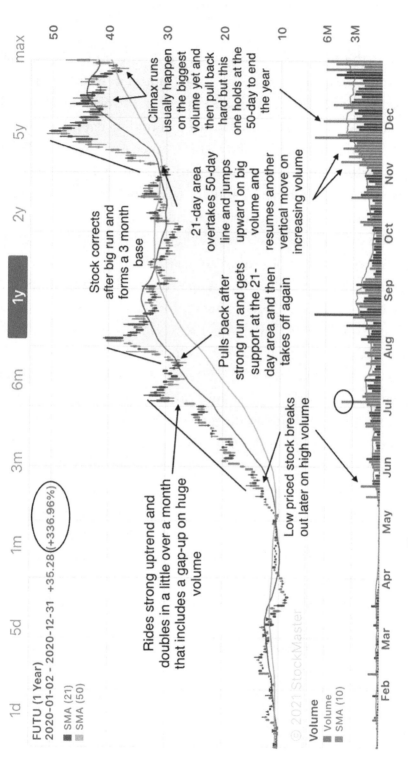

Figure 1-23 Futu Holdings. 2020 Daily Chart. (StockMaster)

In fact, as the months went on, it seemed more leaders were coming out. That is a sign of a very strong uptrend. And the diversity from different sectors of stocks leading was a strong signal as well. Another show of strength was the string of trading days in a row registering positive readings on the H/L/G. Since April 9, when H/L/G turned positive (and the uptrend began), ending 33 straight negative trading days since February 24, there were only 4 trading days of a negative reading within the next 103 trading days until September 4. And those four negative days were light (highest was -170), and they all quickly returned to positive readings.

Some of the new leaders that stepped up in those summer months included Roku, Inc. (ROKU), Square, Inc. (SQ), Zscaler, Inc. (ZS), Farfetch Limited (FTCH), Nio, Inc. (NIO), Tesla, Inc. (TSLA), Growgeneration, Corp. (GRWG), Sailpoint Tech Holdings (SAIL), Digital Turbine, Inc. (APPS), Pinterest, Inc. (PINS), and Fiverr International, Ltd. (FVRR) among others. FVRR was actually an early leader in the spring, but it really started to take off during the summer months. You can clearly see the number of breakout leading stocks growing and representing prior leading sectors like e-commerce, software, and digital payments and new sectors contributing such as EV autos (the two featured offered up some of the best gains of the year) and a marijuana grower. Tesla (TSLA) and Nio (NIO), from the EV group, were big winners for many traders. TSLA was a favorite, offered up many opportunities, and ended up supplying the bulk of large gains for several of the top traders for the year. The rally in the market was strong and gaining power. That window of opportunity was just what monster stock growth traders wait for and then take advantage of.

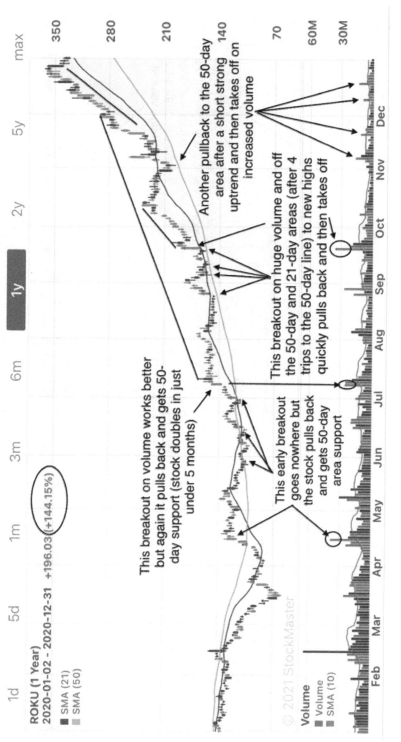

Figure 1-24 Roku, Inc. 2020 Daily Chart. (StockMaster)

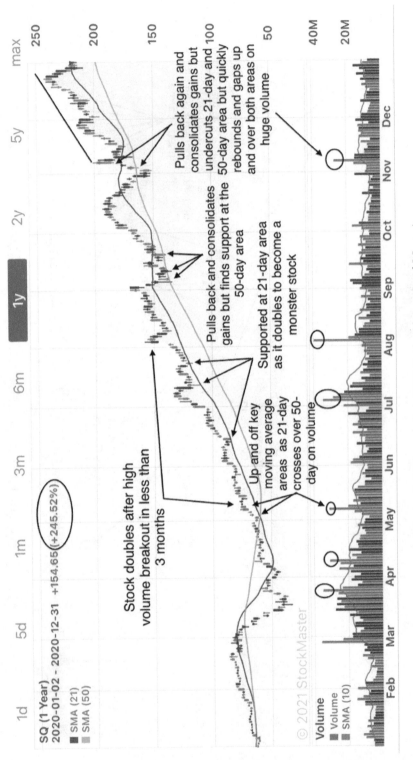

Figure 1-25 Square, Inc. 2020 Daily Chart. (StockMaster)

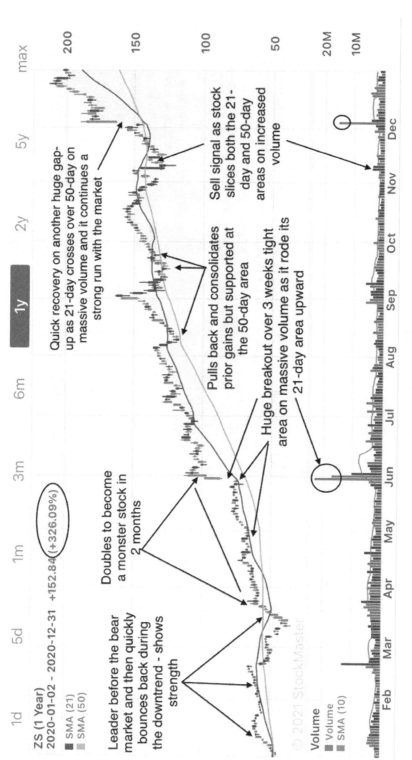

Figure 1-26 Zscaler, Inc. 2020 Daily Chart. (StockMaster)

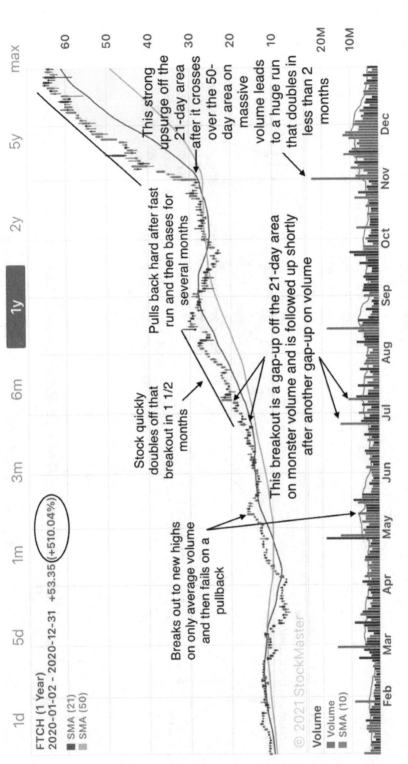

Figure 1-27 Farfetch Limited. 2020 Daily Chart. (StockMaster)

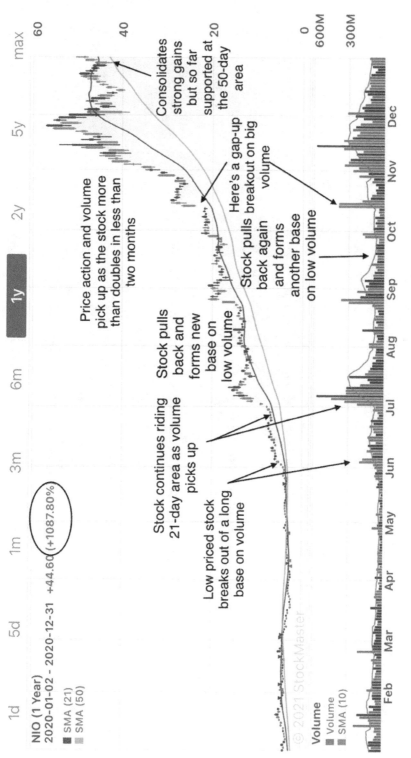

Figure 1-28 Nio, Inc. 2020 Daily Chart. (StockMaster)

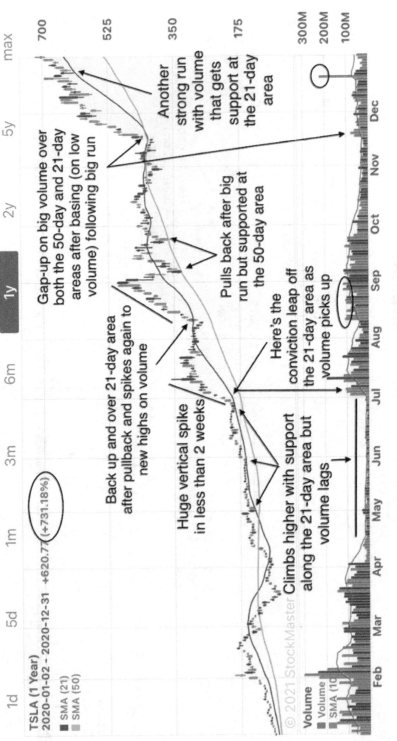

Figure 1-29 Tesla, Inc. 2020 Daily Chart. (StockMaster)

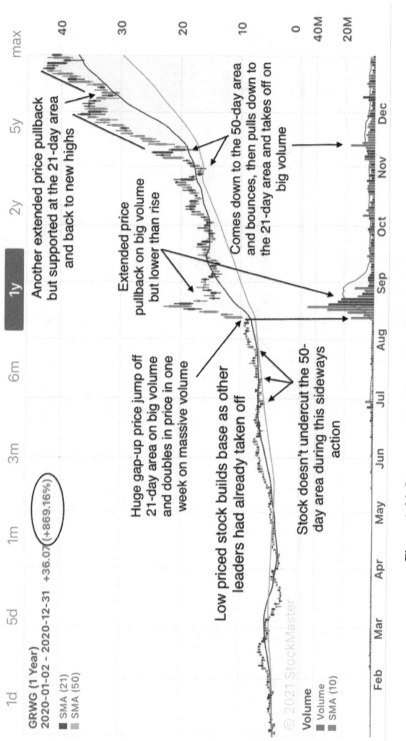

Figure 1-30 Growgeneration, Corp. 2020 Daily Chart. (StockMaster)

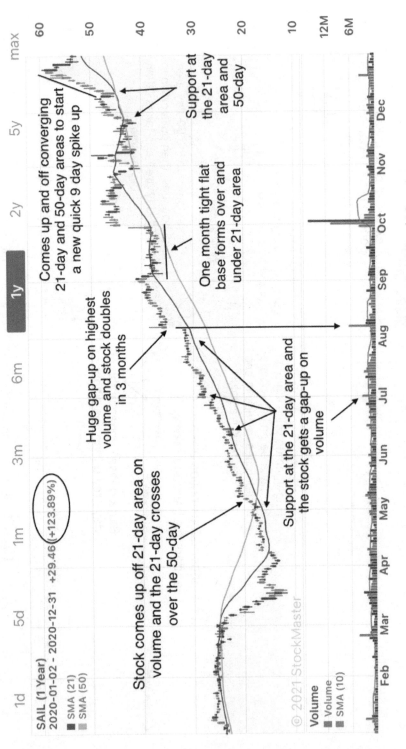

Figure 1-31 Sailpoint Tech Holdings. 2020 Daily Chart. (StockMaster)

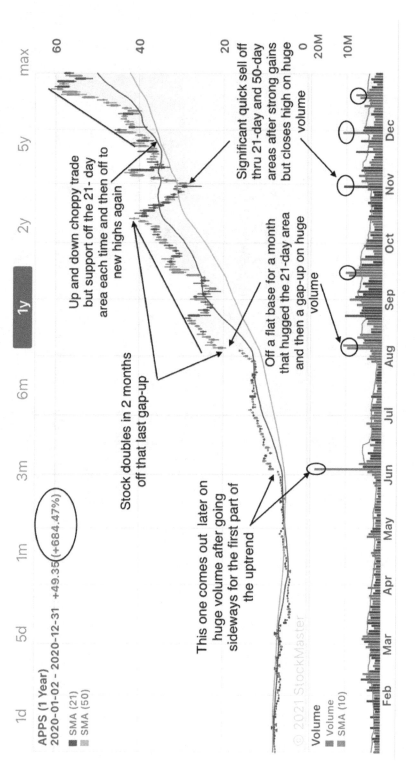

Figure 1-32 Digital Turbine, Inc. 2020 Daily Chart. (StockMaster)

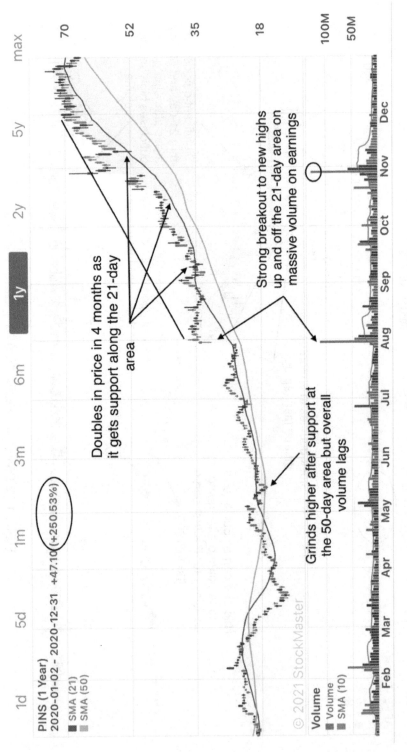

Figure 1-33 Pinterest, Inc. 2020 Daily Chart. (StockMaster)

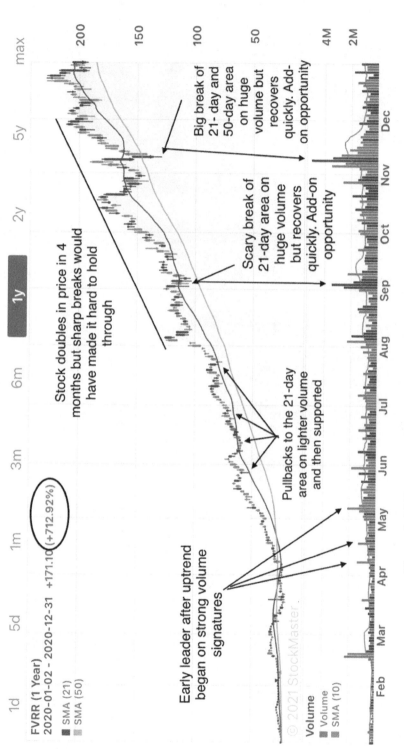

Figure 1-34 Fiver International, Ltd. 2020 Daily Chart. (StockMaster)

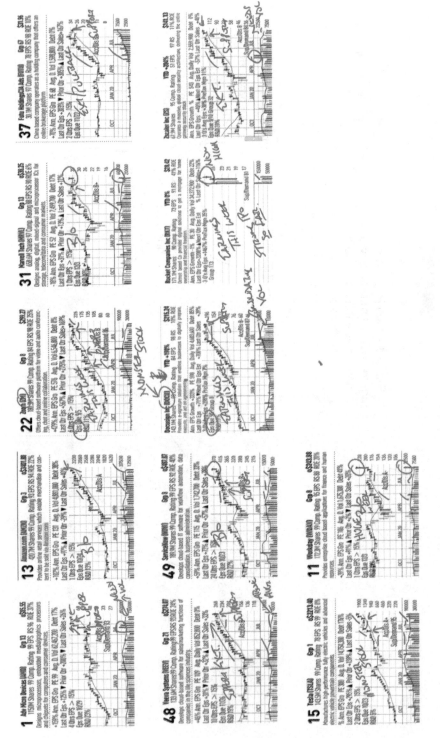

Figure 1-35 Weekly Chart Watchlist. August 28, 2020 Daily Chart. (*IBD*)

Near the end of August, with the market rally in full gear, figure 1-35 is a watchlist from August 28 that show many of the leaders still going strong along with additional names. But on September 4, the H/L/G went negative (just slightly at -43) and broke an impressive 78 trading day positive streak. The next day was negative as well. On September 8, *IBD* downgraded their market outlook to "uptrend under pressure." That was the first change since the "market in confirmed uptrend" upgrade back on April 2. After a few weeks of mostly minor selling, *IBD* then downgraded to "market in correction" on September 23 for just the second time in 2020. The week of September 21 was also the first time since early April that the H/L/G was negative for at least five trading days in a row. But as soon as that occurred, the market turned right back around, and on September 30, *IBD* upgraded their market outlook to "market in confirmed uptrend." Most leading stocks just pulled back in normal fashion during the month of September.

October was a solid month in most regards. Some leaders who scored very strong gains prior to the beginning of fall began pulling back. That is not unusual after many months of solid gains. The last week of October once again saw the H/L/G go negative for five days in a row, just like the prior month. On October 30, *IBD* once again downgraded the market to "market in correction" just after changing to "uptrend under pressure" on October 26. But just like the month before, the market turned right back around and gapped-up several days in a row. On November 4, *IBD* upgraded their outlook back to "market in confirmed uptrend." A few more leading stocks started to really take off during the last few months, and many others already featured bounced off support areas to finish the year strong. Two other strong stocks at the time included Snap, Inc. (SNAP), a social media camera and video company, and The Trade Desk, Inc. (TTD), a cloud-based advertising services firm—both tripled in 2020.

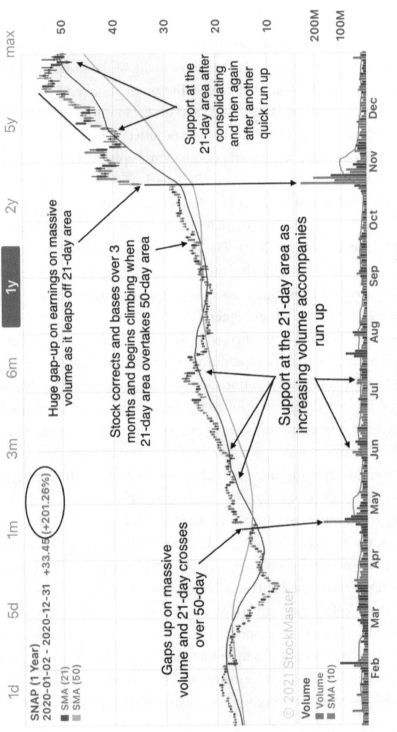

Figure 1-36 Snap, Inc. 2020 Daily Chart. (StockMaster)

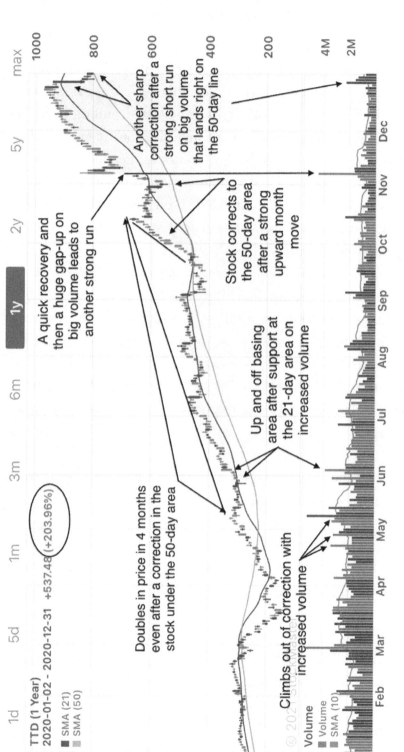

Figure 1-37 The Trade Desk, Inc. 2020 Daily Chart. (StockMaster)

Figures 1-38 and 1-39 are two more watchlists. The first is from October 23 and the second from November 27. You can see more rotation, stocks that came off highs and started pulling back, and some new names. The list is not all inclusive, but it helps to keep up with the weekly charts of leading stocks as the clues are present many times in their price and volume action. Support can be seen, extensions in price, base building, and so on. Doing the homework on a regular basis keeps you in tune with the market, so you can capitalize on opportunities when they arise.

November and December were strong months in the market with the three main indexes finishing the year right at or near highs. And the H/L/G was positive for every trading day during those two months, finishing the year with a strong 42-day positive streak. The Dow ended up 6.9% for the year. The S&P 500 was up 15.8% and the Nasdaq was the leading index scoring a solid 42.6% gain for 2020. It was truly a window of opportunity for growth stock traders that began in early April and continued for most of the year. But several of the leaders featured in this chapter pulled back during December as the indexes kept climbing. We will see if that was a telltale sign for the coming new year.

The year 2020 turned out to be a very strong year for growth stock traders after the carnage from the quick bear market ended after Q1. That's why it pays to always stay attuned to what is happening in the market. Many times throughout history, the market has changed direction when most people didn't expect it. And many times, uptrends begin after sharp declines when the news is still bad. In the spring of 2020, COVID-19 dominated the news, and the outlook did not look good. Throughout history many of the best opportunities arise as the market comes up off a major decline and begins and sustains a new uptrend. Those traders who protected capital

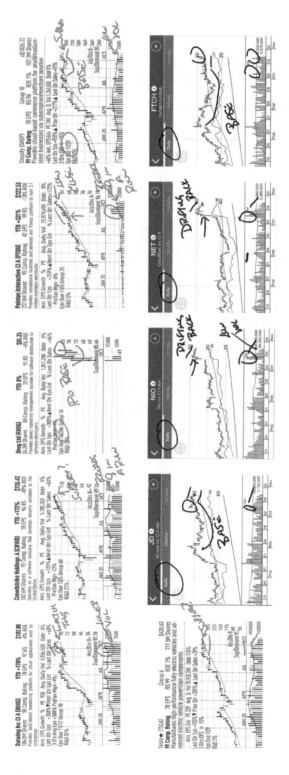

Figure 1-38 Weekly Chart Watchlist. October 23, 2020 Daily Chart. (*IBD*)

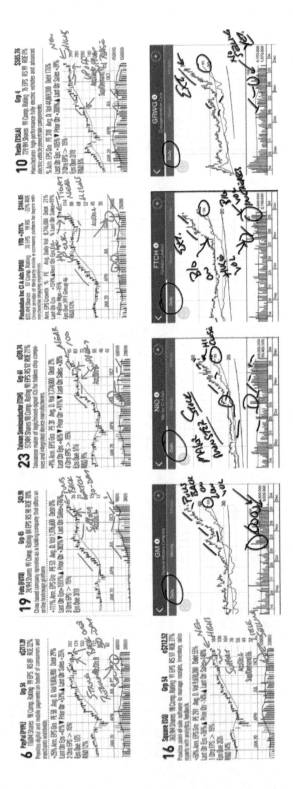

Figure 1-39 Weekly Chart Watchlist. November 27, 2020 Daily Chart. (*IBD*)

Monster Stock Lessons

Figure 1-40 Dow Jones Index. 2020 Daily Chart. (StockMaster)

Figure 1-41 S&P 500 Index. 2020 Daily Chart. (StockMaster)

Figure 1-42 Nasdaq Index. 2020 Daily Chart. (StockMaster)

during the quick bear market and came back into many of the stocks that setup early and then reached monster stock status did very well. Most of the big movers were listed on the Nasdaq, but there were several sectors that did well. There were twenty-nine monster stocks featured in this chapter that more than doubled. Of those, twenty-two at least tripled in price. That's quite a bit in one year. No trader gets them all. But it only takes a few big winners in a year, if handled correctly and losses are cut short on your losing trades, to have a solid year.

Many top traders scored triple-digit gains in 2020 by getting into several of the leading stocks featured in this chapter and riding them up when the uptrend began in the spring. Then they sold many of them either into strength or when they showed classic topping or selling signals. Each year there is a U.S. Investing Championship contest. There are different divisions, and George Tkaczuk had an impressive year leading the managed account division with a 119% return.

2020 STANDINGS (124 Entrants)

Performance through December 31, 2020

MONEY MANAGER VERIFIED RATINGS ($1 MILLION+ Accounts)

STOCK DIVISION

George Tkaczuk + 119.1%

Bill Roller + 15.2%

Here are the top five traders from the 2020 U.S. Investing Championship in the individual stock division ($20K minimum).

UNITED STATES INVESTING CHAMPIONSHIP

STOCK DIVISION

Oliver Kell + 941.1%

Tomas Claro + 497%

Ryan Pierpont + 448.4%

Matthew Caruso + 346%

Shahid Saleem + 322%

Top Traders

Oliver Kell set a new record in the competition with his incredible 941.1% return. Some of Oliver's biggest winners included Tesla (TSLA, figure 1-29), Fastly (FSTY, figure 1-21), and Livongo Health (LVGO, figure 1-16). He got in LVGO early at around $25 in March as it held up well during the heavy selling and was viewed as assisting people in a new COVID-19 world. He sold a portion of his shares when they were up 50% but he held the core position. He then sold out completely at $135 soon after the merger was announced in August. That core position returned 440%. He traded FSLY several times with his best run on it from $29 to $95 for a 226% return in two months. He swing traded it several other times and was also caught (along with many other top traders) in the big gap-down in mid-October. He quickly sold out his position then instead of hoping for a comeback and did not trade the stock again. TSLA was a major winner for Oliver. He swing traded in and out of that leader throughout its great run. He started early, in March, while the market was still falling. He was stopped out then but came right back in near the end of March when the heavy selling started to abate. He then started building positions near $100 and pyramided add on buys up through $117. He ran those up quickly to near $150 and then sold out on a negative reaction to earnings. He came back in again near $145 and made additional pyramid buys near $170, $200, and $205 as the stock was taking off on a strong run. He piled into this leader with a huge position—somewhere near 70% of his total account. That is serious concentration and something top traders throughout history have done when they know they're right. He ended up selling major portions of his total holdings at $325 and then more at $300. He was stopped out for a small loss in August as the stock pulled back and consolidated its gains. But TSLA came screaming back, and Oliver rebought it near $300 and held that position until he sold it near $475 and $450 for a combined quick 55% return. In September and November, he was stopped out for some small losses trading it again. But one loss hit him hard—he bought on September 4 at $395 and sold it at the open on September 8 for a 10% loss. That's cutting your losses, but he was heavily concentrated with 40% of his account in that position. Those losses can take a toll, but he was up so much by this point in the year that he took that risk. That trade didn't work, but it didn't deter him either. In mid-November, TSLA started to take off again, and Oliver really piled in. He left that prior loss behind him, and he still had conviction in this stock since it was really starting to run. He went in heavily again and concentrated his position (again near 70% of his total account). He took positions near $462 and added positions up through $500 and then held those at year end when TSLA closed 2020 at $705. He then ended up selling those positions out in early 2021 near $875. Please review the TSLA chart closely in figure 1-29, and you can then trace Oliver's trades to that chart to see how a top trader returns over 900% in one year! He also did well in TWLO (figure 1-19), ROKU (figure 1-24), and DDOG (figure 1-17) just to name a few. Oliver wrote a book called *Victory in Stock Trading* that came out in 2021, which details his trading strategy. I highly recommend it. You can follow Oliver on Twitter @1charts6.

Matt Caruso, who placed fourth in the stock division with a remarkable 346% return, landed several of the stocks featured in this book. Three of his best trades were also in LVGO and FSLY, along with The Trade Desk (TTD, figure 1-37). For LVGO, Matt started buying on April 3 at $28.50. That was right near the beginning of the market uptrend. He ended up selling his positions on August 5 at $144.00 when the buyout merger was announced. That was a four-month average gain of 405%! He bought FSLY on May 7 at $27.50. That was the stock's first breakout gap-up. He sold his positions on October 14 at $91.00. That was a five-month average return of 231%. He bought TTD on April 22 at $232.00. That was just weeks after the market had confirmed an uptrend, and more stocks started to breakout and lead. He sold TTD on July 14 at $430.00 for a quick three month return of 85%. He had many other successful trades throughout the year, and he always cuts short his losses when they went against him. You can follow Matt on Twitter @Trader_ mcaruso. Matt offers a one-time subscription video service for all levels of traders from beginner to expert. It's an excellent course, professionally done, and quite extensive with video and charts included. It's well worth the one-time subscription price.

Ryan Pierpont returned an incredible 448% to place third in the stock division. He also placed third in 2021 (please see Chapter Two). Ryan's strategy is a swing trading approach, so he holds positions for only a few weeks or so. But he latches onto the true leaders and then swing trades through and around them. It's critical to suit a trading strategy to fit each individual's needs and personality. Ryan's best trades in 2020 were in TSLA. He bought shares in early April as the market was beginning its uptrend and TSLA was coming up the right side of a base on volume. He sold that position in early May for a quick, strong gain. He then came back into TSLA in early July when the stock made a new high off the 21-day area on big volume. That move led to a vertical spike (seen on figure 1-29) for several weeks. Ryan sold his position right into that strength for a big, solid short-term gain. He came back in again in mid-August after a short pullback and then it ripped higher again for a few weeks. Ryan once again sold that position into strength in early September for another strong short-term gain. He did this type of trading one more time in

2020 with TSLA. In November he bought it again and rode its fast rise into early December for another strong gain. He did miss that last strong move throughout the month of December and into 2021, but he scored major gains with TSLA using a strategy that he has perfected for himself. As mentioned, Ryan came back again in 2021 to place third once again in the stock division, using his swing trading strategy of buying liquid strong leaders off key buy point areas and then selling them into strength and repeating the process.

Jim Roppel, who I've written about before and who manages Roppel Capital Management, had a triple-digit return in 2020. A few of his big winners were ZM (figure 1-6), ROKU (figure 1-24), and TTD. Eve Boboch is a portfolio manager and market strategist at Roppel Capital Management. The fund Eve manages also earned a triple digit return in 2020. Her best trade was also TSLA. She traded TSLA many times in 2019 as well, but in 2020 she really hit a home run with this stock. It was her largest position, and she concentrated heavily in it because it was the true market leader, and it was leading the market in 2020 during the uptrend. Concentrating heavily in one or two stocks when the market is right and you're in one of the best leaders was a key strategy of William J. O'Neil. Back in 2003, O'Neil had a highly concentrated position in eBay. He knew the company's story, the fundamentals were top notch, and he scored a huge gain on the stock. Eve knew Tesla well, and she followed that same concentrated strategy. Her initial position in TSLA was in early October 2019. She did very well with the stock then but sold out completely in February 2020 due to both Tesla's parabolic move and the deteriorating market conditions. As the 2020 uptrend was gaining momentum, she came back into TSLA on May 18, 2020 at $165.86 (split adjusted). She swing traded around that core position many times during the remainder of the year. She added, trimmed, and so on when conditions such as earnings announcements were imminent or other extensions or support targets presented themselves. By mid-January 2022, that core position was up 532%.

Eve's next big trade in 2020 was Peloton (PTON, figure 1-8). Eve's buy and sell transactions on PTON are textbook monster stock transactions. Eve started buying PTON on April 13 at $29.79 right near the beginning of the market uptrend. She added or pyramided her position several times in June and traded around that initial core position several more times as conditions warranted it. She reduced exposure when her core position was up over 70%. Eve made additional buys in late September as the stock really started to make a move. As it took off on a vertical run, she sold positions into strength in mid-October. She made several other trades in the fall of 2020, and she exited her remaining position in PTON on April 20, 2021 at $105.55. That core position in the stock netted her a return of 254%. You can follow Eve on Twitter @EBoboch. Eve coauthored *The Lifecycle Trade*, which was published in 2018 and is a top selling book on IPOs and growth stocks.

You can see these top traders made big gains on several of the same stocks. That's because those stocks were the standout leaders during the year, and they offered several opportunities during their strong runs. And leading stocks get the attention of top traders. Even though each trader's strategies differed, they all recognized these stocks and then applied their strategy to each. Several of the traders would take a core position in a leader, and as long as it kept working, they would then sell or trim a portion of the position into strength. If the stock broke hard, like FSLY did, they sold out the entire position. But many would swing trade around their core position. And they cut their losses short on those swing trades if they didn't work. The successful swing trades added to their gains while keeping them in their core positions for larger overall gains.

Chapter Two – 2021

The market started the new year where 2020 ended. As the uptrend continued, many leaders from 2020 bounced off support areas that were tested near the end of that year. A few other new candidates started to make moves as well. But the best performers continued to be several of 2020's monster stocks. But not all of them. Some broke hard and lost their leadership status. Those hard sell signals need to be heeded to cut loose when it's time to let go. FSLY was one of the first to go back in October 2020 (see figure 1-21). That hard sell off caught many traders by surprise. But the stock never recovered from that classic sell signal. ZM was another stock (figure 1-6) that lost its leadership status in the fall of 2020. When sharp breaks below the 21-day and 50-day areas occur, especially on big volume, and then those areas become resistance instead of support, those are classic sell signals. Typically, if the stock doesn't recover quickly, those breaks solidify a change of trend has occurred in that stock. We will view many more of those in the next chapter—Lessons Learned. That's why when it's time to cut loose, one does so. You don't want to give back a majority of the profits you earned on a successful transaction. There will always be other opportunities.

January continued the uptrend, but by the end of the month, on January 29, *IBD* changed its market outlook to "uptrend under pressure." But just as quickly, the market turned around and resumed the uptrend on February 2. That action was similar to 2020 when the

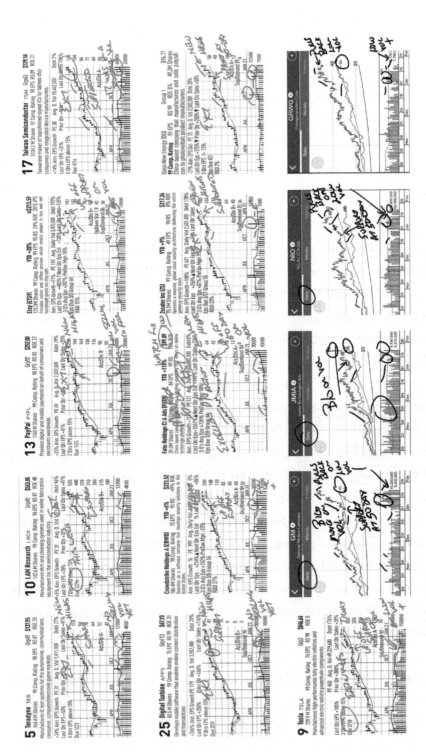

Figure 2-1 Weekly Chart Watchlist, January 23, 2021 Daily Chart. (*IBD*)

uptrend went to market under pressure but quickly righted itself. The weekly watchlist in figure 2-1 showed that many of the leaders continued providing opportunities with very few offering up major sell signals, such as the ones we saw with FSLY and ZM. The uptrend was gaining strength, and most of the leaders from 2020 kept their uptrends intact, and several new candidates were offering new opportunities with healthy basing patterns.

February kept the uptrend going but the H/L/G was registering net-positive numbers in the +900 range by midmonth. Past history has shown those levels to be excessive and unsustainable over the intermediate term. By the end of February, *IBD* again put its market call at "uptrend under pressure," and on March 4 they went further by downgrading it to "market in correction." The market once again rebounded quickly, and on March 10 it was upgraded to "uptrend resumes." But there was a subtle change going on in the market. In mid-March we start to see clues of sector rotation occurring. That change would end up defining the theme of the market for most of 2021. Growth stocks that soared for much of 2020 started to lose some traction, and new breakouts would begin to be short-lived. Follow-throughs on classic breakouts started to slip, and it started to became more of a trader's market (more adaptable to swing trading, scalp trading, and even day trading). Even though many leaders and the market indexes didn't correct much, many stocks started to trade in a choppy fashion. And leadership was changing. More defensive sectors and economic recovery stocks started to lead. Figure 2-2 is a watchlist of leading stocks from late March.

Other stocks that were showing promise in early spring of 2021, that eventually became monster stocks that year, included ZIM Shipping Services (ZIM), Devon Energy Corp. (DVN), Nucor,

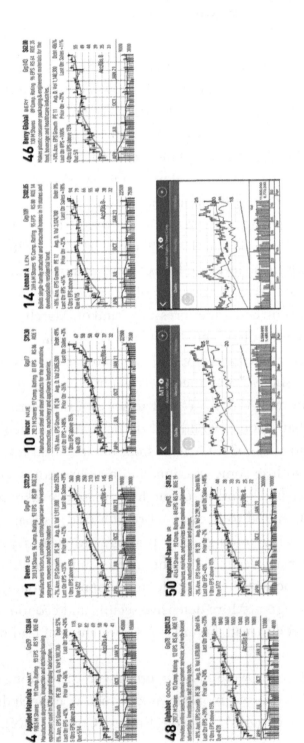

Figure 2-2 Weekly Chart Watchlist. March 29, 2021 Daily Chart. (*IBD*)

Corp. (NUE), and Diamondback Energy, Inc. (FANG) among others. ZIM was an IPO that went public near the start of the year. From the watchlist in figure 2-2 and the stocks just mentioned (with charts below), you can see the rotation to other sectors taking place. From shipping to energy to steel, the expansion in the market was growing, but it was narrowing for individual stock traders that were used to the high-growth stock environment that 2020 offered. Many of those high flyers were pulling back as rotation started to become more prevalent. One stock that stood out, though, was Fortinet, Inc. (FTNT), an IT security firm. FTNT looked like one of the monster stocks from 2020 with its steady rise. Another high flyer from the start was Futu Holdings (FUTU) that was featured in Chapter One. FUTU blasted upward in short order but then succumbed to selling pressure after its climax run.

The market turned back around in early April, and many prior growth technology leaders that pulled back found support and continued their runs. Other sectors continued coming up but then pulled back as quick sector rotation started to become more commonplace. But the market was churning leaders—one week it was one particular group, and another week the market was rotating to something else. Though the markets trend was up and the H/L/G stayed positive the entire month of May, it was getting difficult to hold leaders who came up and off basing patterns. Breakouts occurred during the uptrend, but following up on those was becoming very challenging. The market was showing signs of a very different environment from the 2020 market. The months of May, June, and July saw *IBD* change their market outlook eight different times. It went from "uptrend under pressure" on four different days to "uptrend resumes" on four different days as well, the last within that three-month timeframe being July 23. Scattered throughout were

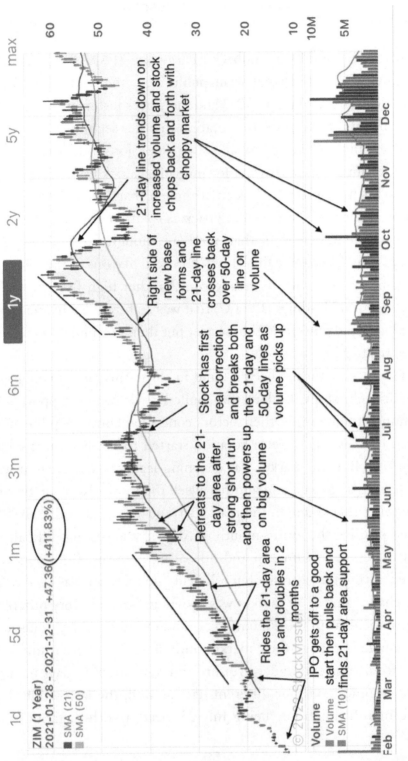

Figure 2-3 ZIM Shipping Services. 2021 Daily Chart. (StockMaster)

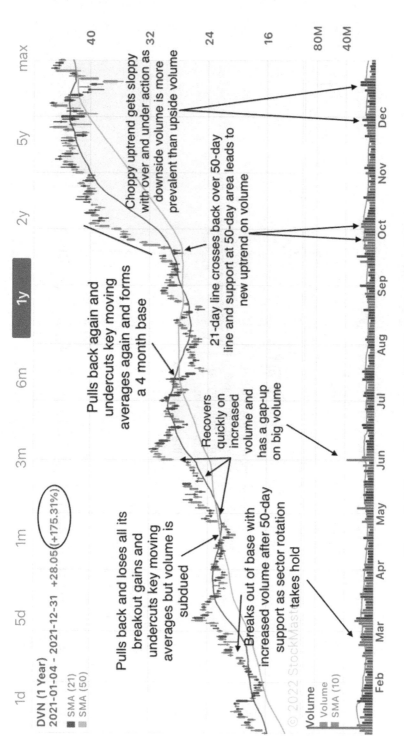

Figure 2-4 Devon Energy, Corp. 2021 Daily Chart. (StockMaster)

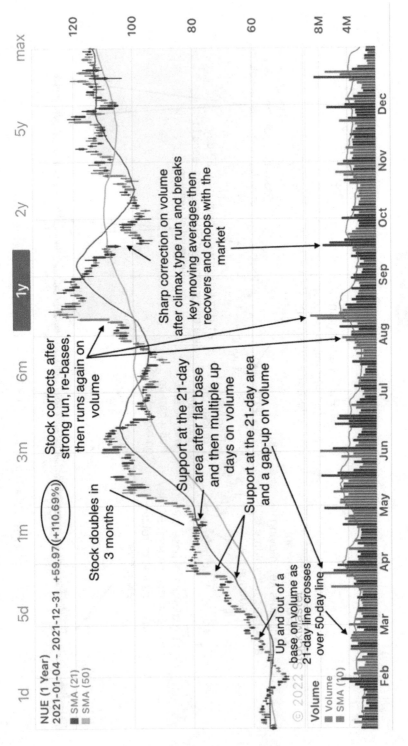

Figure 2-5 Nucor, Corp. 2021 Daily Chart. (StockMaster)

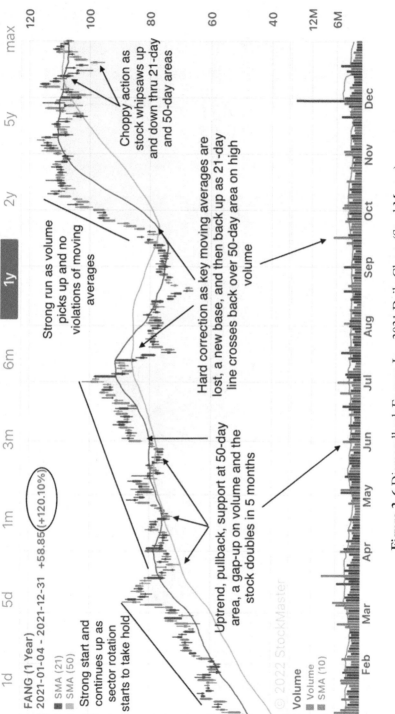

Figure 2-6 Diamondback Energy, Inc. 2021 Daily Chart. (StockMaster)

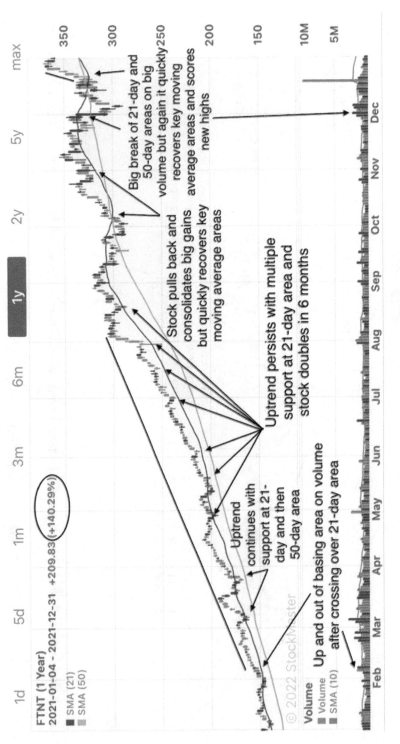

Figure 2-7 Fortinet, Inc. 2021 Daily Chart. (StockMaster)

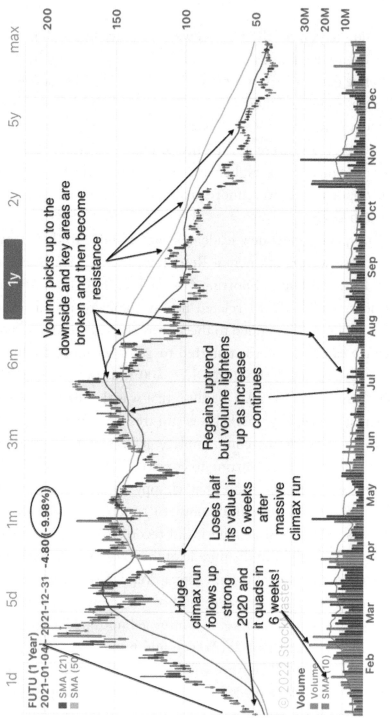

Figure 2-8 Futu Holdings. 2021 Daily Chart. (StockMaster)

nine trading days were the H/L/G went negative but with no trend to those negative readings. Trends to the H/L/G typically start with three to five days in a row going in either direction. Those key stats prove what a choppy environment the market had become, especially when you compare it to a strong uptrending market like the one in 2020. There were still plenty of opportunities as the overall market kept moving higher and making record highs. It's just that the opportunities were more profitable to a shorter-term swing trading approach.

In late spring, a few new leaders began or added to their moves. Among those were Continental Resources, Inc. (CLR), BioNTech SE (BNTX), and Dick's Sporting Goods, Inc. (DKS). Another energy leader, a COVID-19 related health company, and a leading sporting goods reseller added to the sectors showing leadership. But as summer came, the market started to get a bit more choppy, as figure 2-12 displays. I chose the S&P 500 Index to include *IBD*'s market change calls for 2021 because that was the leading index as far as performance. The market was still trending upward, but with sector rotation becoming commonplace, it became more challenging as prior leaders were starting to correct.

August was another somewhat choppy month as the market turned back around after midmonth to resume an uptrend. The H/L/G was mostly positive, but it did record five days in a row of negative readings right in the middle of that month. When it turned positive again, the market resumed its uptrend. Also, August was the first month of the year that *IBD* did not change their overall market outlook—it stayed "market in confirmed uptrend." Figure 2-13 is a watchlist from August 27. You should notice that some of the monster stocks from 2020 were still leaders and getting some fresh attention after building bases from consolidating prior gains. A few

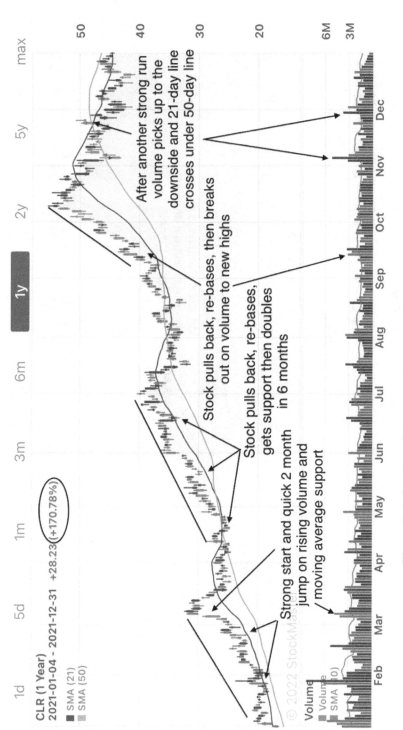

Figure 2-9 Continental Resources, Inc. 2021 Daily Chart. (StockMaster)

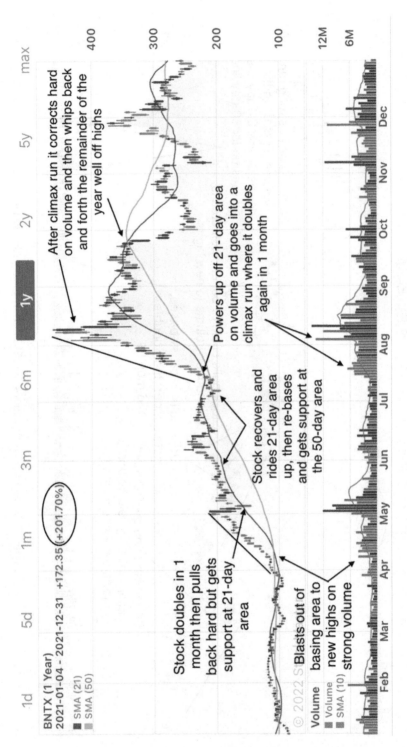

Figure 2-10 BioNTech SE. 2021 Daily Chart. (StockMaster)

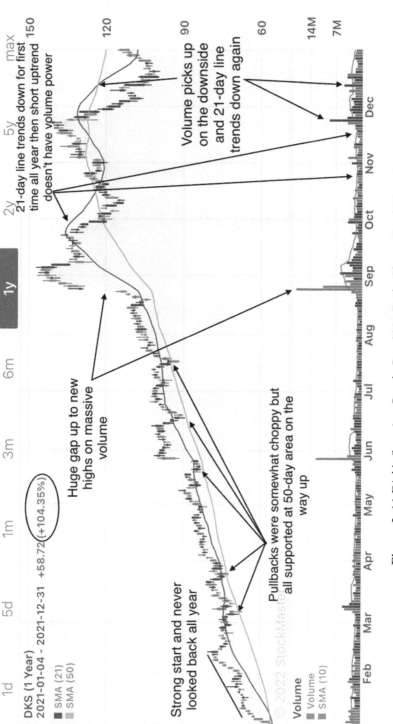

Figure 2-11 Dick's Sporting Goods, Inc. 2021 Daily Chart. (StockMaster)

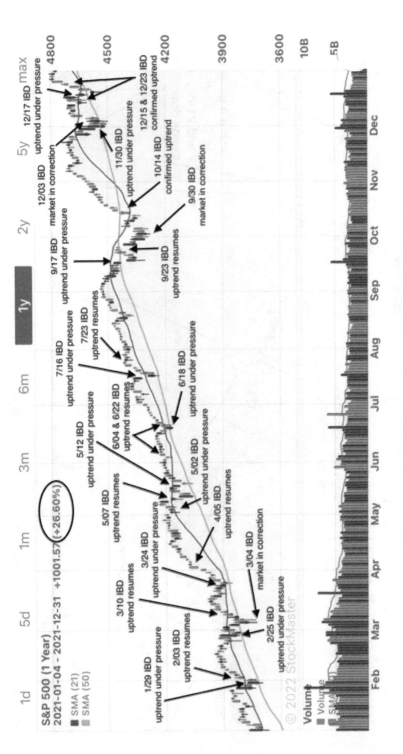

Figure 2-12 S&P 500 Index. 2021 Daily Chart. (StockMaster)

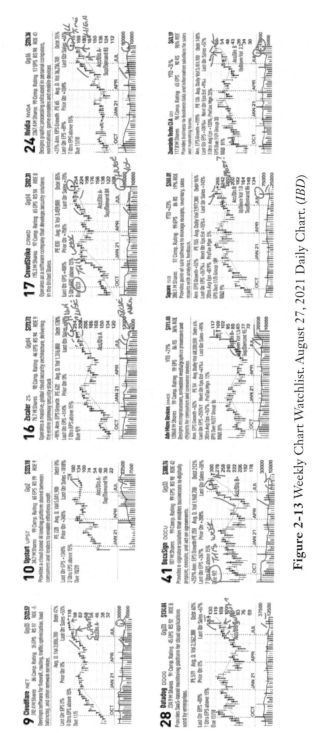

Figure 2-13 Weekly Chart Watchlist. August 27, 2021 Daily Chart. (*IBD*)

of the best were NET, ZS, and DDOG. Another was TSLA. A few more leaders started to come out, including Nvidia, Inc. (NVDA), the graphic processing unit leader. But as some prior leaders continued on, others faltered. Some of those from 2020 that started showing selling signals and started to trade in a more volatile, choppy fashion were CRWD, PYPL, and TWLO. A few of them wobbled badly before breaking decisively to the downside.

A few other leaders started making moves in mid to late summer. Asana, Inc. (ASAN), Moderna, Inc. (MRNA), Upstart Holdings, Inc. (UPST), and InMode, Ltd. (INMD) were added to the leaders list. A software technology company, another COVID-19 health firm, an AI lending company, and an Israeli cosmetic health company were some of the more notable stocks making progress. ASAN started moving in early June. UPST, which was included on the watchlist in figure 2-13, built a very tight, flat base across the summer months and then took off in early August on a huge climax run. MRNA was mirroring BNTX in many ways as both firms were fighting COVID-19 with vaccine solutions. MRNA broke out in early June and basically ran straight up for two months in another stock marking a climax run. Climax runs are great opportunities to sell into strength. The best traders over history kept their euphoric emotions under control and used climax fast runs as sell signals. Many amateur traders buy into climax runs that are extended, which causes the climax run that the seasoned traders use to sell into.

The fall months brought more choppy trading. September was a down month, and within it, *IBD* changed their market outlook four times. The fourth change was to "market in correction" on the last day of September. The H/L/G had also gone negative for three days in a row by then. The beginning of October was no better as the negative H/L/G stretched to seven days in a row by October 6, the longest losing streak of the year up to that point. But by October 14,

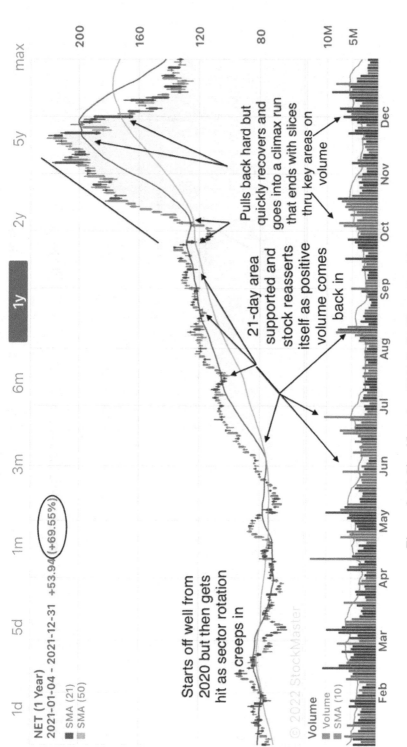

Figure 2-14 Cloudflare, Inc. 2021 Daily Chart. (StockMaster)

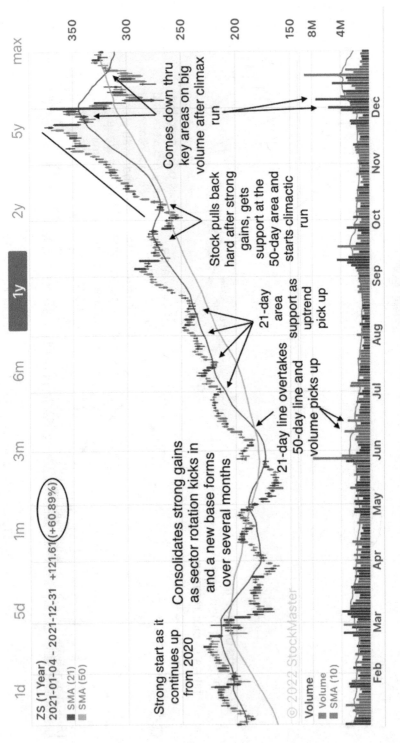

Figure 2-15 Zscaler, Inc. 2021 Daily Chart. (StockMaster)

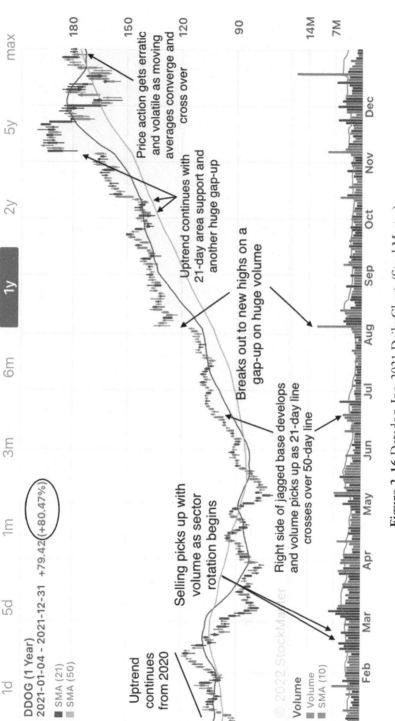

Figure 2-16 Datadog, Inc. 2021 Daily Chart. (StockMaster)

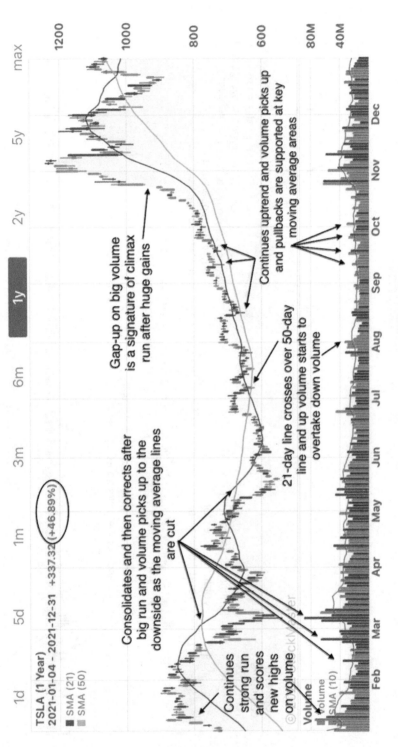

Figure 2-17 Tesla, Inc. 2021 Daily Chart. (StockMaster)

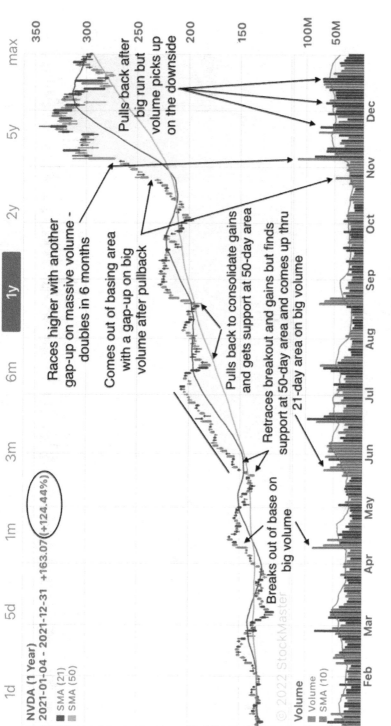

Figure 2-18 Nvidia, Corp. 2021 Daily Chart. (StockMaster)

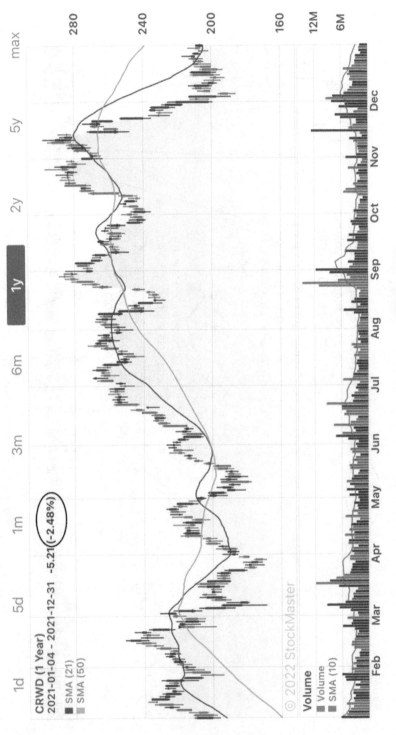

Figure 2-19 Crowdstrike Holdings. 2021 Daily Chart. (StockMaster)

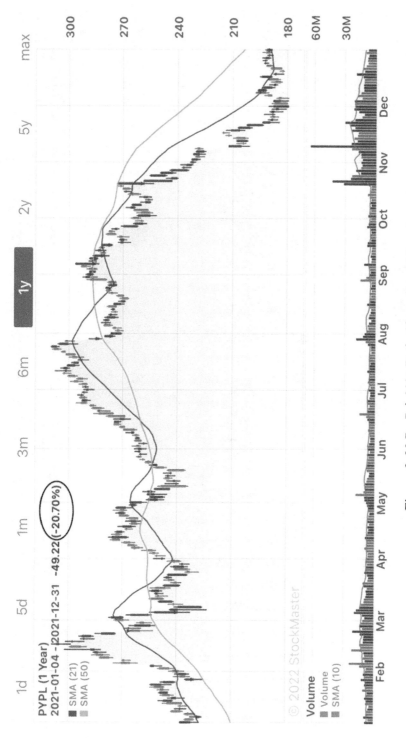

Figure 2-20 PayPal. 2021 Daily Chart. (StockMaster)

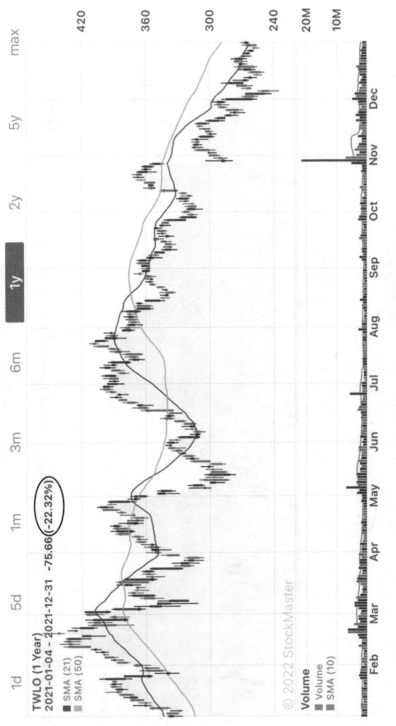

Figure 2-21 Twilio, Inc. 2021 Daily Chart. (StockMaster)

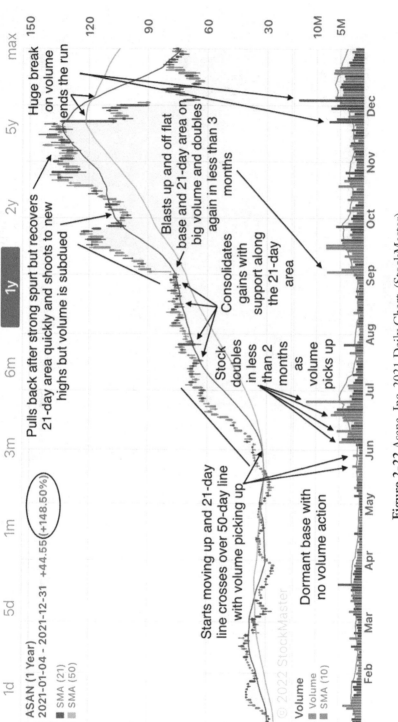

Figure 2-22 Asana, Inc. 2021 Daily Chart. (StockMaster)

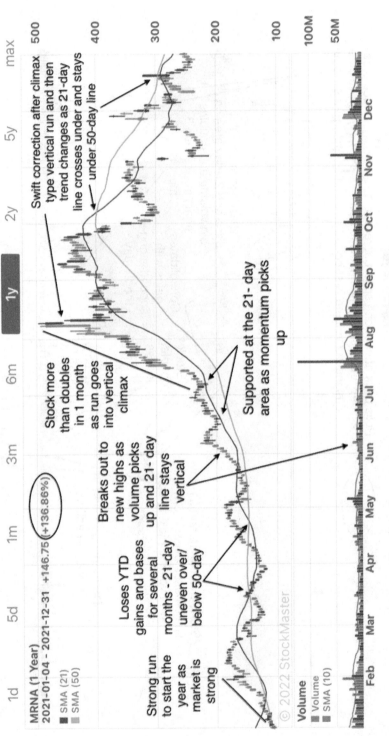

Figure 2-23 Moderna, Inc. 2021 Daily Chart. (StockMaster)

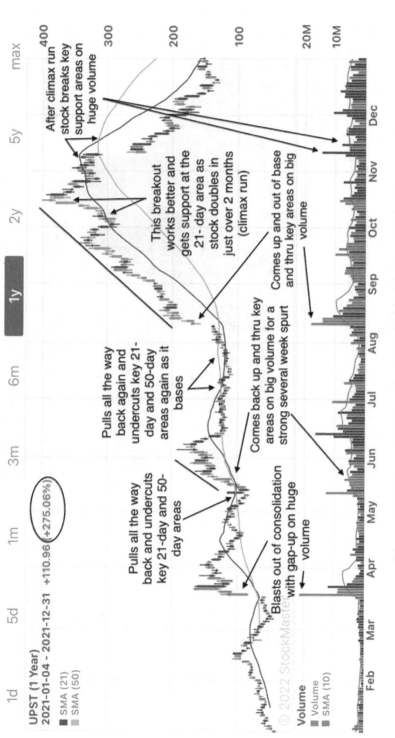

Figure 2-24 Upstart Holdings, Inc. 2021 Daily Chart. (StockMaster)

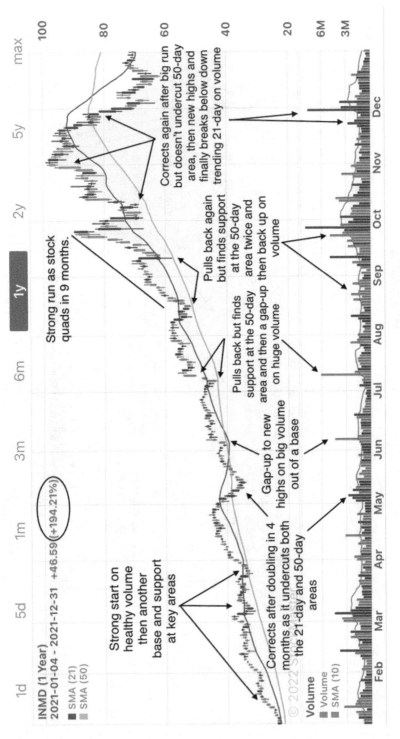

Figure 2-25 InMode, Ltd. 2021 Daily Chart. (StockMaster)

the market was moving higher, the H/L/G was positive five out of the last six trading days, and *IBD* upgraded their market call to "market in confirmed uptrend." Both the S&P 500 and The Dow retook their 50-day moving average lines. The next day, the Nasdaq did as well. And, most importantly, leading stocks started moving up on volume. The watchlist of strong RS and fundamentally strong (either past, current, or anticipated) stocks was growing too. Figure 2-26 is a watchlist from October 15. Watchlists consist of leaders in price action with volume accompanying that action, along with stocks setting up in bases or finding support at key areas.

As the market continued its uptrend, a few more leaders took off on strong runs to finish the year. Builders FirstSource, Inc. (BLDR), ON Semiconductor, Corp. (ON), and Arista Networks, Inc. (ANET) were a few of those producing strong, short upward runs into the end of the year. A housing market stock, a semiconductor firm, and a cloud-based network technology company added to the mix of leading stocks. All three of them had gap-ups at the beginning of November on strong volume, which is a buy signal. And all three stocks had strong two-month surges from those early November gap-ups through December that accounted for the best part of each of their gains for the year. That shows that only getting a portion of a monster stock move during the year can improve one's performance and returns for that year. And all three stocks were in uptrends and proved to be leaders before those late year gap-ups occurred.

A nice six-week rally ensued that saw the markets rise from that October trend change. That uptrend was basically uninterrupted, and the H/L/G ran positive for twenty-five straight trading days in a row. But by mid-November, the market started to show selling distribution and choppiness returned. The H/L/G turned negative on November 17 and then dominated over positive readings the rest of the year. On

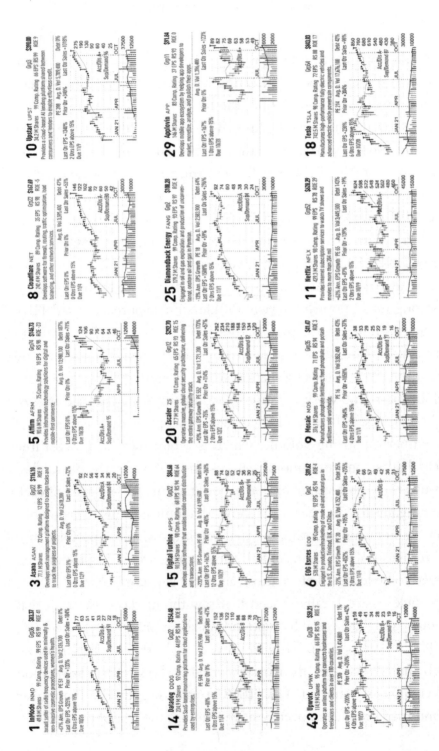

Figure 2-26 Weekly Chart Watchlist. October 15, 2021 Daily Chart. (*IBD*)

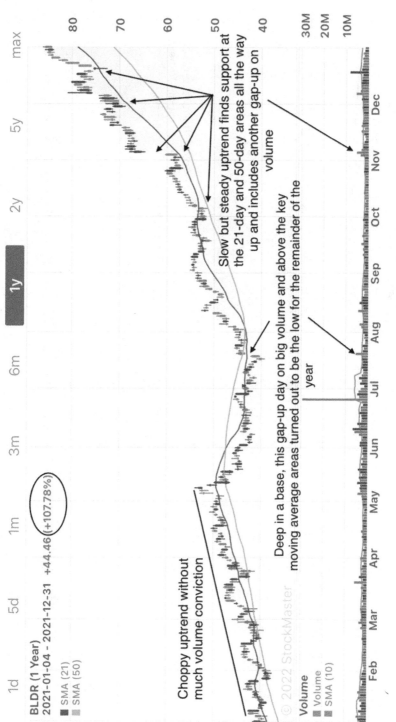

Figure 2-27 Builders FirstSource, Inc. 2021 Daily Chart. (StockMaster)

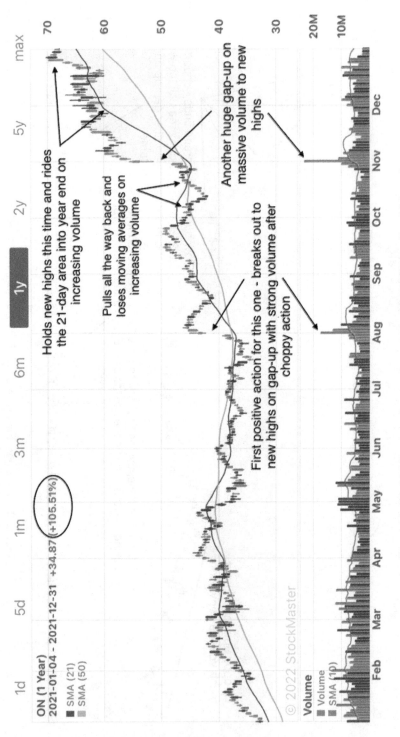

Figure 2-28 ON Semiconductor, Corp. 2021 Daily Chart. (StockMaster)

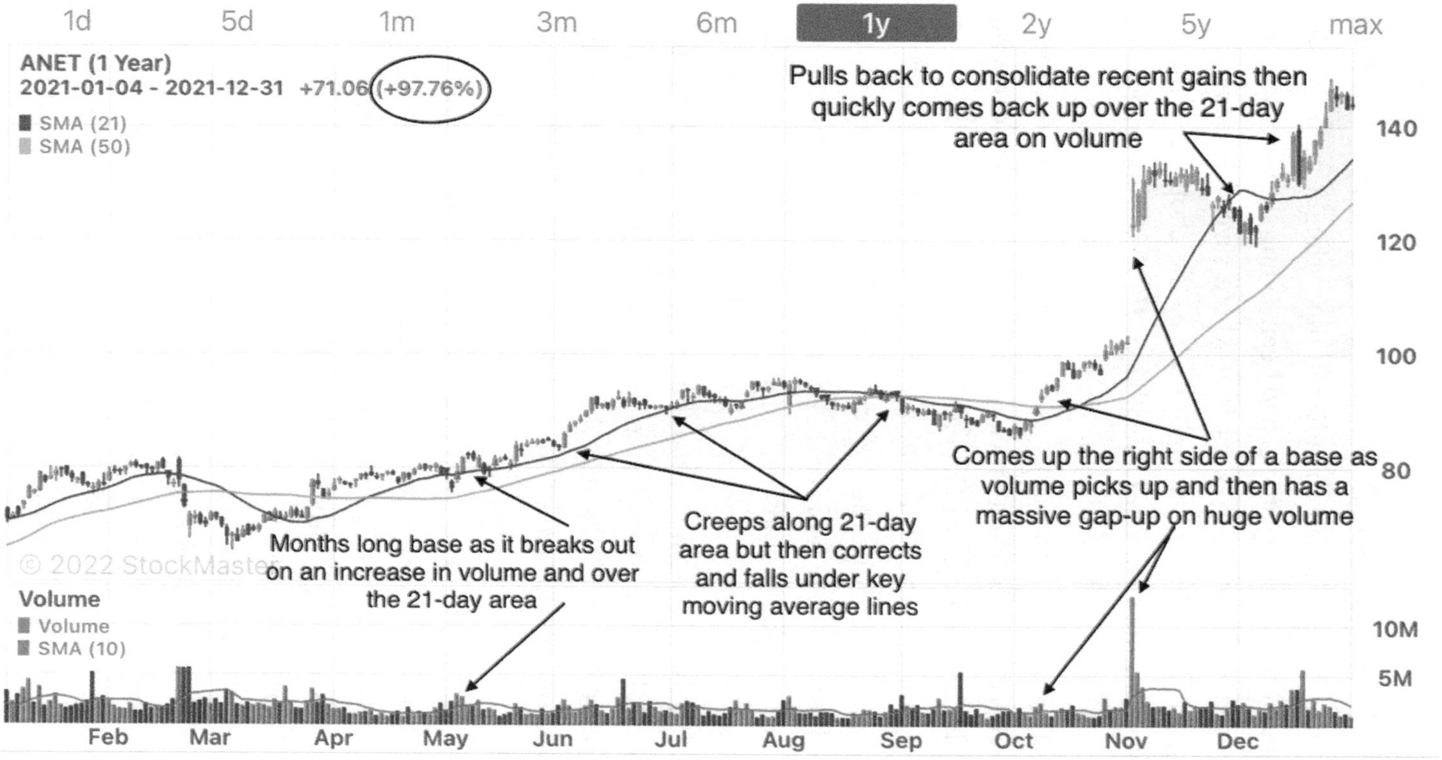
1d
5d
1m
3m
6m
1y
2y
5y
max
ANET (1 Year)
2021-01-04 - 2021-12-31 +71.06 (+97.76%)
SMA (21)
SMA (50)
Pulls back to consolidate recent gains then quickly comes back up over the 21-day area on volume
140
120
100
80
10M
5M
Comes up the right side of a base as volume picks up and then has a massive gap-up on huge volume
Creeps along 21-day area but then corrects and falls under key moving average lines
Months long base as it breaks out on an increase in volume and over the 21-day area
© 2022 StockMaster
Volume
Volume
SMA (10)
Feb
Mar
Apr
May
Jun
Jul
Aug
Sep
Oct
Nov
Dec

Figure 2-29 Arista Networks, Inc. 2021 Daily Chart. (StockMaster)

November 30, *IBD* downgraded the market to "uptrend under pressure," but the H/L/G had already run nine straight trading days in a row negative, and leading stocks had been selling off for a week or two by then. After that nice six-week run where several breakouts began working, in December it was right back to the choppiness that dominated much of the year. On December 3, *IBD* went to "market in correction." Many of the leaders from the mid-October rally had been selling off, and sector rotation was coming back in play, but the selections were limited (the three stocks just featured were a few that bucked the distribution trend). On December 15, *IBD* switched back to "confirmed uptrend," but two days later they again switched to "uptrend under pressure." But one thing that stayed consistently negative was the H/L/G. It then turned positive on December 23, the same day *IBD* upgraded their market outlook to "uptrend resumes." That was the fourth change in the market direction call by *IBD* in December. The market then ended the year with a decent burst the last week of the year.

The S&P 500 Index was the leader of the major indexes with a return of 26.6% for 2021. The Nasdaq scored a 20.7% return, and the Dow Jones Index ended up 18.7%. There were sixteen monster stocks featured in this chapter that more than doubled (I did include ANET with a 98% return) in 2021. Of those, only three tripled or more. Those totals were much less than in 2020 from the stocks featured in Chapter One. Even though the major index returns were solid and close to each other in performance, the number of monster stock leaders was significantly smaller. That's not unusual after a big year like 2020. But as an uptrend ages, it gets more challenging. We saw that with the number of market call changes from *IBD* and the back-and-forth reading on the H/L/G. You can see how many times the reading went negative (below the median line in figure 2-33) when compared to 2020 in figure I-3 from the Introduction.

Monster Stock Lessons

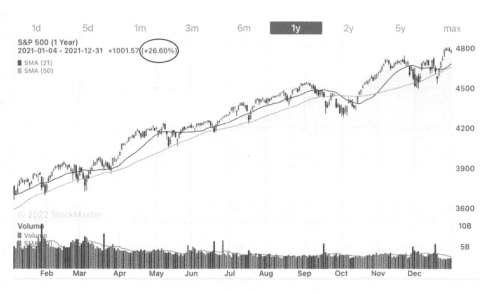

Figure 2-30 S&P 500 Index. 2021 Daily Chart. (StockMaster)

Figure 2-31 Nasdaq Index. 2021 Daily Chart. (StockMaster)

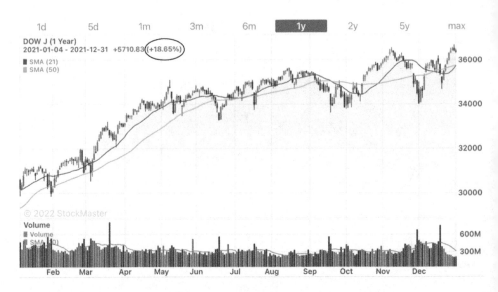

Figure 2-32 Dow Jones Index. 2021 Daily Chart. (StockMaster)

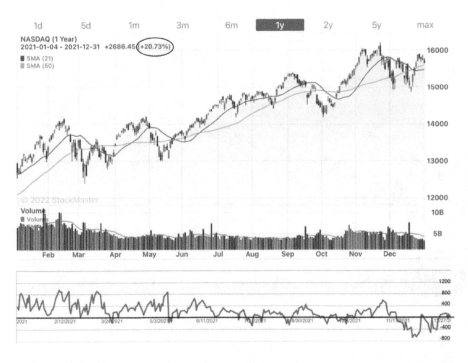

Figure 2-33 Nasdaq Index 2021 & Net New Highs to New Lows. (StockMaster)

Top Traders

Top traders still outperform in more challenging markets. In the U.S. Investing Championship contest for 2021, there were a handful of top performers that produced triple-digit returns.

Mark Minervini took first place overall with an impressive 335% return in the money manager stock category, which was a record for that division. That was Mark's second time winning the contest. He also won in 1997 with a return of 155%. Mark has been one of the most successful individual traders over the past three decades. In 2020, he did not enter the contest, but ended up producing another triple-digit return of 150%. Mark was featured in Jack D. Schwager's *Stock Market Wizards* book and is a best-selling author who has written three top selling books. Please see my book recommendations in the conclusion where I rank two of them among the best stock market books ever written. You can follow Mark on Twitter @markminervini. He offers an annual workshop that many of the yearly top traders in the stock division have attended. Mark also offers a subscription service where traders can follow his successful strategies in real time.

2021 STANDINGS (338 Entrants)

CURRENT MONTHLY STANDINGS

Performance through December 31, 2021

(Past performance is no guarantee of future results)

MONEY MANAGER VERIFIED RATINGS ($1 MILLION+ Accounts)

STOCK DIVISION

Mark Minervini + 334.8%

Vibha Jha + 100.4%

Hsiu-Ping Peng + 11.4%

Here are the top five performers from the 2021 Stock Division (minimum $20K account).

UNITED STATES INVESTING CHAMPIONSHIP

STOCK DIVISION

Pavel P. Sterba + 222.3%

Roy Mattox + 214.4%

Ryan Pierpont + 201%

Brandon Warnock + 133.4%

WM Kerry Brown + 106%

Ryan Pierpont repeated his third-place performance again in the stock division. Ryan's swing trading strategy once again served him well in 2021 with an impressive 201% return. He swing traded several Chinese stocks that were leaders in the early part of the year. EHang Holdings Limited (EH) and Up Fintech Holdings (TIGR) were two of his biggest winners. He bought Fluent Genetics (FLGT) toward the beginning of the year near $50 and sold it late in the month at near $90. Ryan bought TIGR at the beginning of the year and sold it in early February after it already quadrupled in a little over a month. He also bought FUTU (figure 2-8) at the start of the year over $40, but he took a strong short-term gain near $60. He missed that huge climax run that can be seen in the chart as it more than quadrupled to $200 by mid-February. That climax run turned out to be the high for FUTU as it then started a fast descent. Ryan bought EH in early February near $70 and sold it a few weeks later after it quickly ripped higher to just under $130. Other successful trades throughout the year generated around 10% short-term gains. That quick trading with shorter term gains reiterates how much more challenging the time period from March to the end of the year 2021 turned out to be. Larger intermediate term opportunities were getting scarce as the uptrend chopped its way higher until year end. You can follow Ryan on Twitter @RyanPierpont.

Roy Mattox came in second place in the stock division with a very impressive 214% return. Roy is also more of shorter-term swing trader. Recall that the market in 2021, especially from February to the end of the year, rewarded shorter-term traders over position traders. Roy traded many of the stocks featured in this book including LVGO, ZM, FSLY, DDOG, and UPST among others. Roy was trading in the leaders; he just tightened up his time frames in order to take advantage of what the market was offering. He scored many 20% gains throughout the year, trading inside those leaders from that shorter time frame. It pays to trend with the market, and Roy proved that by generating a great return in 2021. You can follow Roy on Twitter @RoyLMattox.

Chapter Three –
Lessons Learned

The years 2020 and 2021 in the stock market—both up years for the major indexes but very different in several ways. Many of the lessons learned from both years can help one in future market cycles. Much of the activity for each year was similar to other market cycles before. There will always be differences, but some key measures do repeat themselves. It's been that way for many decades, and it will likely occur again in the future due to human nature. The following are some of the chronological lessons learned along the way during those two years.

Lesson #1

The first lesson was about being observant to all the negative signals that were becoming prevalent in early spring of 2020. COVID-19 was one of those events that threw nearly everything into uncertainty and panic, to some degree. Stocks started topping, the indexes were experiencing distribution on increasing volume, the H/L/G was going negative, and *IBD* had downgraded the overall health of the market. When those four measures go in those directions, it is time to play defense. It was time to sell stocks and go to the sidelines with all the negative signals flashing. Those more experienced could have shorted the indexes or the leading stocks that exhibited classic sell signals. But more than anything, that short but powerful bear market decline was a lesson in defensive selling skills. Cutting losses short and not trying to go against the trend of a market in a clear downtrend are timeless lessons in the market. It was also a lesson in capital and mental preservation. Nothing is more important in the market than preserving capital when the market begins and continues on in a downward trend. That way, when the market turns around, which it always does, you will be in a healthy capital and mental state to take advantage of the next uptrend and the opportunities it will offer.

Lesson #2

The next lesson learned was about having the ability to wait out a market decline until clear signals show that the decline may be ending. That is a skill of patience learned from experience over time. Being patient adds to capital preservation, which goes a long way in protecting your capital and, more importantly, your mental capital capacity as well. Not getting frustrated during a market decline or getting whipped up and down from the volatility inside one goes a long way in keeping your emotions intact, so you can be ready for the next market uptrend. Time out of the market gives you time to review your past mistakes and read and reread excellent market books to continually educate yourself, as the market is a never-ending learning process. Patience is such an important part of the discipline required that, when practiced and implemented, goes a long way, especially if you plan to be involved in the market in the long term.

Lesson #3

If you followed the first two lessons in early 2020, then the next lesson was about being prepared for a new uptrend when the time comes. Still doing chart work and reviewing weekly watchlists keeps you engaged and on top of the skills needed when things turn around, which they always do. Not getting discouraged and giving up will allow one to take advantage of the next opportunities that come along. And you saw how many opportunities arose during that strong April through August uptrend in 2020. Stocks that declined the least and held up and showed relative strength (RS) during downtrends are typically the best candidates to become leaders when the market begins a new uptrend. Homework is required no matter what the market is doing. Top traders have a disciplined approach to their routines. They keep up the research work no matter what condition the market is in. The difference between their results and others is in executing on their research. If conditions are not ideal, they don't do anything. Many top traders think a cash position in a downtrend is as important as being in leading stocks during an uptrend. And if conditions change, they are ready to pounce and get involved. It's all in the preparation that comes from the work required to stay on top of things, no matter what the current conditions may be.

Lesson #4

Getting engaged and involved when the market turns around, especially after a major correction or bear market period, no matter how long it lasted, is the next lesson. Many times (most people won't believe it) that is when the best early opportunities will present themselves. Trending lightly at first helps to get a feel for any ensuing uptrend. *IBD* has a very reliable record for calling the beginning of uptrends. Just review the market charts to see those (figures I-1 and 2-12). No one knows if a new attempted uptrend will last, which is why you make test or pilot buys to check its validity. If the attempted rally begins to fail, you bail. The one in early April

2020 is the one that stuck. Also, tracking the H/L/G (along with the *IBD* calls) is very beneficial. If the H/L/G starts to rebound and trend positively after a big market decline, that can be the sign of a market turning. But most important is the quantity and quality of strong fundamental stocks that resisted the decline, the best with rising relative strength (RS) lines, and solid bases that were built during a declining market. Those stocks tend to break out first and lead when an uptrend begins and sustains. The key lesson here is to get engaged in the market with pilot buys in the stocks you've researched during the decline that begin to move. If you've protected your financial and mental capital during the down market, then you will be in a better position (both financially and mentally) to get involved. If you took some hard hits because of hesitation or denial, which can happen to anyone, then you won't be ready in both capital capacities to perform at your best. And that early time in an uptrend is when the best opportunities begin. All the best traders in history that I've researched found that when markets turn up from a correction and that uptrend persists is when they started to score their best returns.

Lesson #5

If lessons one through four were adhered to in the spring of 2020, and you're back in the market, the focus then turns to your strategic risk management control and trading strategies in handling any leaders that were purchased along the way. Key growth stock trading strategies include strict loss control when a trade goes against you, initialing pyramiding up on strength, selling strategies from both the offensive and defensive side, and buybacks up and off key moving average areas or within basing patterns. Keeping your risk strategies to plan and keeping your mental processes controlled are key traits. Each person should have their own strategic plan that fits their personality. We saw differences at the end of Chapter One and Two in some of the top traders. Their strategies differed to fit their particular style, but their results were similar. Whatever your strategies and defined edges are, discipline is the key. Having the discipline to stick to your successful plan will lead to consistency.

We will look at a few of the monster stocks from 2020 while pointing out some classic buying and selling points and also see how they fared in 2021. Remember, two of the first stocks out in 2020 during the April uptrend were ZM and DOCU. Their business products and models were in high demand due to the new COVID-19 work-from-home environment. However, even though they gave many top traders strong gains during 2020, those two stocks also gave classic selling signals after their big runs. It's important to know how and when to sell in order to realize the profits you earned. The following two charts will be replicated from earlier but with additional areas pointed out for the best possible buy/add opportunities (in blue) and sell/trim opportunities (in red) in 2020. You can go back to the charts in this book and look for similar instances with all of them. That is actually a good practice and research project for each reader. Later in the chapter, I will show ZM and DOCU again with their 2021 daily charts as well, so you can clearly see why selling strategies are key to retaining profits in big leaders. The last thing you want to do is round trip a big gain in a leader you handled correctly but then froze and ignored selling tactics to retain the profits you had earned.

Buy/add opportunities will usually be the following:
Breakouts from basing areas—preferably on big volume

Gap-ups on big volume

Power pivots within a base on volume

Bounces off support areas of either the 21-day and/or 50-day area—on volume is best

Sell/trim opportunities will usually be the following:

Gap-downs on big volume

Climax runs

Extensions in price over 21-day and/or 50-day areas (offensive sell tactics)

Breaks of prior support areas of the 21-day and/or the 50-day areas on big volume (defensive sell tactics)

I'll summarize the steps from *Monster Stocks* that historical big leaders all had in common, that many of the stocks featured in this book followed, and that match the two just discussed:

- The Setup—waiting patiently for the market to confirm a trend. The beginning of uptrends typically brings out the best leaders that set up the best bases during a correction.
- The Breakout—breakouts out of sound bases on increased volume are clear buy signals.
- After the Breakout—pyramid buys on the initial burst up often pay off if the uptrend persists and the stock follows suit. Support moves off key moving average areas after pullbacks are also additional buy opportunities. Failed breakouts should be cut short to minimize losses.
- The Run-Up—selling into strength after extensions from key moving average areas keeps profits in successful trader accounts. Looking for the climax run and defensive selling

strategies on breaks of key moving average areas on volume are also prudent selling tactics.

Remember the definition of a monster stock at the beginning of the book: "The meatiest part of a fast-advancing monster stock usually occurs between 6 and 12 months of its major move." Many of the best leading stocks in 2020 did make their moves in short order—some did it in only 3 or 4 months! Stocks don't go up forever, so it pays to have sell rules to lock in some of the big gains earned. Selling into strength is probably one of the hardest rules to implement, but top traders throughout history have discovered its importance to their long-term success. Figure 3-1 shows the fast moves of ZM and a few opportunities to sell to lock in some of those strong gains and not give them all back. ZM never reached those 2020 heights in 2021. In fact, for long term holders that hung on, they would have given them all back and more (figure 3-3). Several of those big leaders in 2020 did the same when they round tripped their strong advances.

It's important to note that no one catches all the gains of a monster stock. And no one gets them all by any measure. The objective here is to at least latch onto a few of the biggest leaders the market offers up each year. If you're lucky or good enough to be in a few, then you want to be invested in them for at least a portion of their big move. If your objective of being active in the market is to make money, then why wouldn't you want to be in the biggest movers? Leading stocks increase your odds of success. And we saw in the prior two chapters that some top traders who ranked at the top of the annual U.S. Investing Championships for 2020 and 2021 needed only to make some great moves in just a few of the leaders to score impressive returns for their accounts.

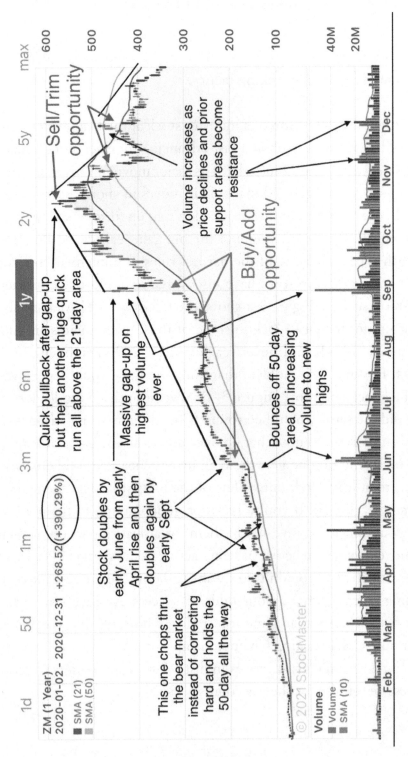

Figure 3-1 Zoom Video Comm. 2020 Daily Chart. (StockMaster)

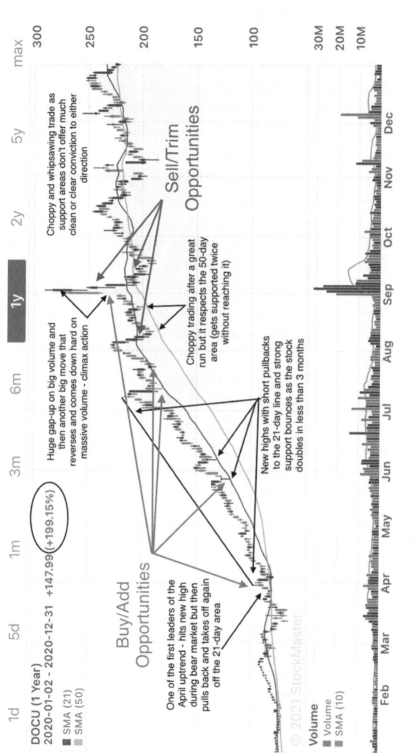

Figure 3-2 DocuSign Inc. 2020 Daily Chart. (StockMaster)

I encourage each reader to go back to each stock featured in this book and mark up some buy/add opportunities and sell/trim opportunities to the charts that would be similar to figure 3-1 and figure 3-2. Or mark up your actual trades in those stocks to see how to improve in the future if you missed some of the big moves. The more you study your past trades and then compare them to past big winners, the more you will start to see where you can improve in the future. There is no better substitute in the market for being honest with yourself by studying what you did, the opportunities you missed, and the mistakes you made. In the market there are no certainties, so everyone makes mistakes—and plenty of them! It's part of this business. But the more you recognize your weaknesses and then correct them in future transactions, the more you'll start to see improved results.

Now we will look at several of the monster stocks from 2020 and compare their price action to their 2021 results. You will see how they topped and started to give warning signs. Many topped in similar fashion. When the trend of a big leading stock starts to change, it's prudent to change with that trend. Having solid sell rules in place will help you act when it's time to act. There are many lessons on buying and selling that one can learn from studying historical charts of past leaders. William J. O'Neil endorsed the cover of *Monster Stocks* with a great quote: "Study past big winners and you'll buy future ones." And he should know better than anyone, as he landed plenty of them during his career. Studying past leaders will help you in the future, both on the way up and on the way down. But nothing beats getting in there and experiencing it as it happens. Make no mistake, it's not easy! Mistakes and losses are the best teachers of all. You need to burn yourself many times to learn to stop actions that don't work. Study the following charts and you'll see when trends changed.

Monster Stock Lessons

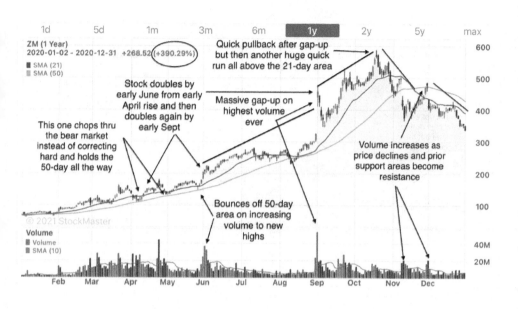

Figure 3-3 Zoom Video Comm. 2020 & 2021 Daily Chart. (StockMaster)

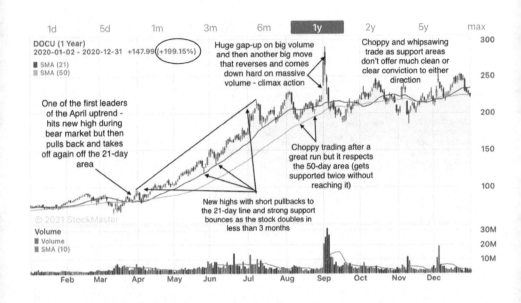

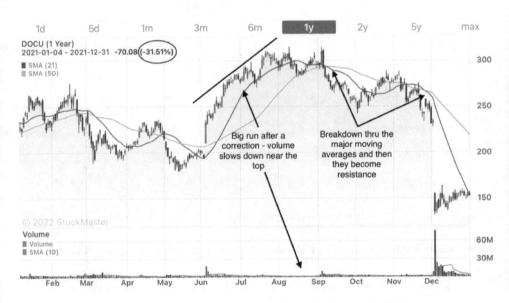

Figure 3-4 DocuSign Inc. 2020 & 2021 Daily Chart. (StockMaster)

Monster Stock Lessons

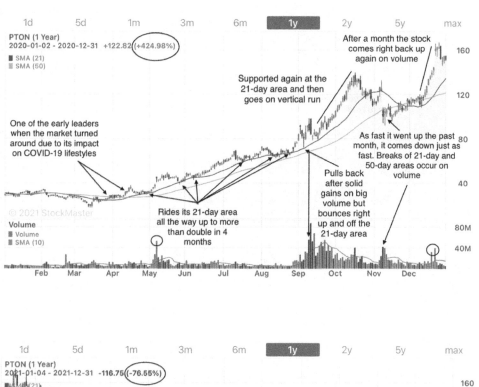

Figure 3-5 Peloton Interactive. 2020 & 2021 Daily Chart. (StockMaster)

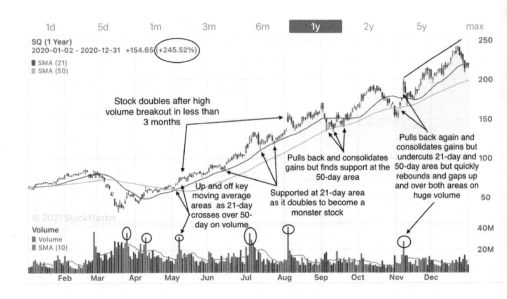

Figure 3-6 Square, Inc. 2020 & 2021 Daily Chart. (StockMaster)

Monster Stock Lessons

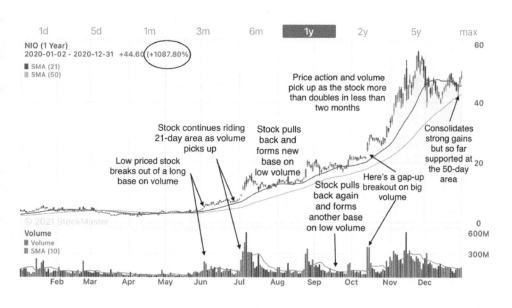

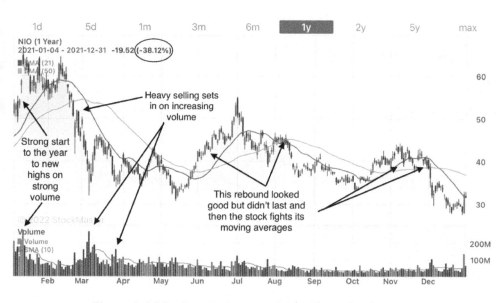

Figure 3-7 Nio, Inc. 2020 & 2021 Daily Chart. (StockMaster)

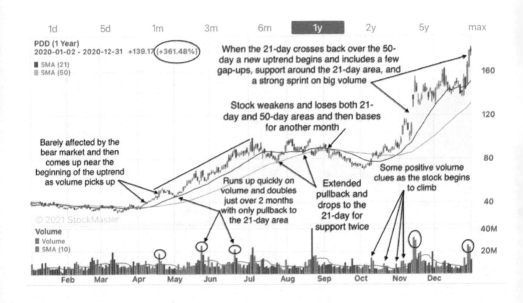

Figure 3-8 Pinduoduo, Inc. 2020 & 2021 Daily Chart. (StockMaster)

Monster Stock Lessons

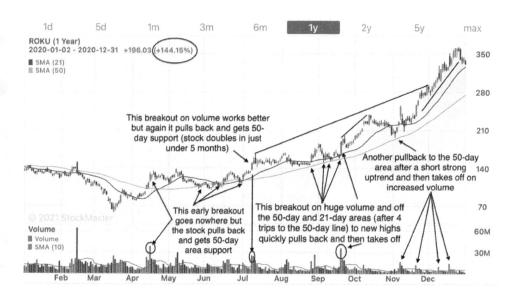

Figure 3-9 Roku, Inc. 2020 & 2021 Daily Chart. (StockMaster)

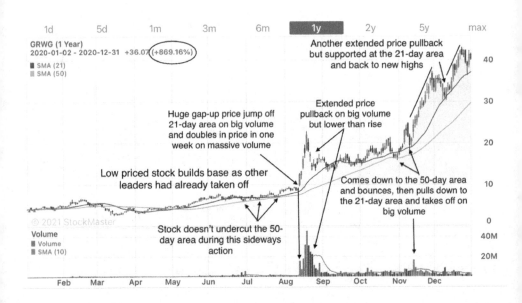

Figure 3-10 Growgeneration, Corp. 2020 & 2021 Daily Chart. (StockMaster)

Monster Stock Lessons

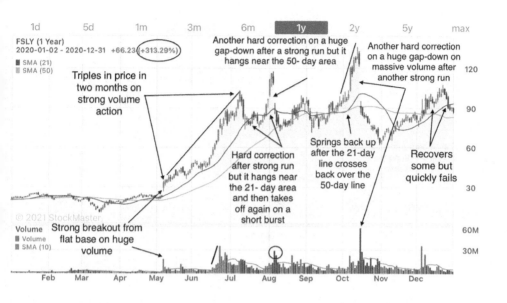

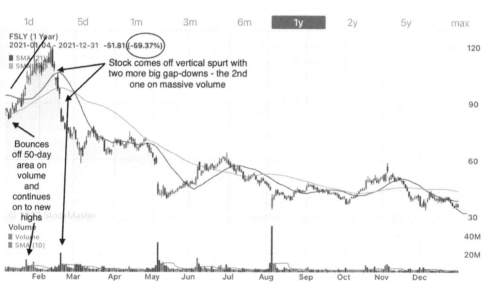

Figure 3-11 Fastly, Inc. 2020 & 2021 Daily Chart. (StockMaster)

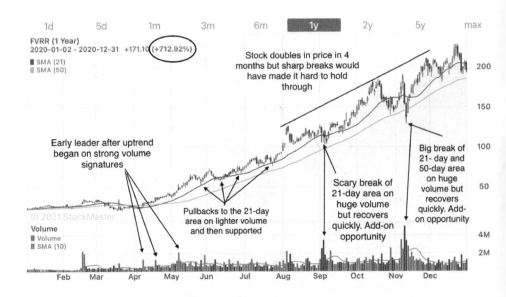

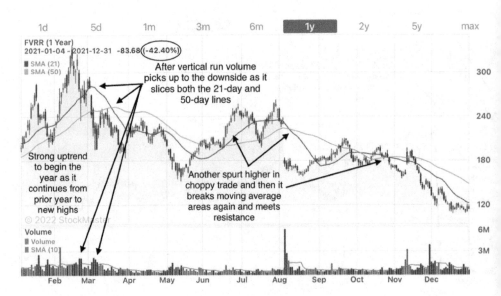

Figure 3-12 Fiverr International, Ltd. 2020 & 2021 Daily Chart. (StockMaster)

Monster Stock Lessons

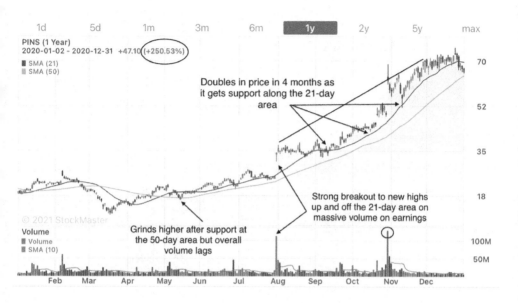

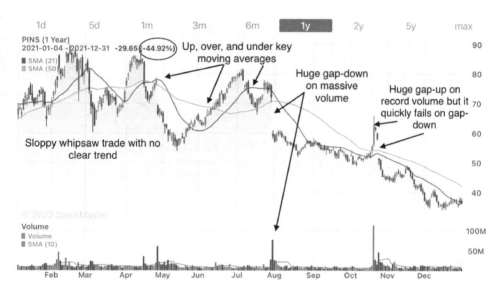

Figure 3-13 Pinterest, Inc. 2020 & 2021 Daily Chart. (StockMaster)

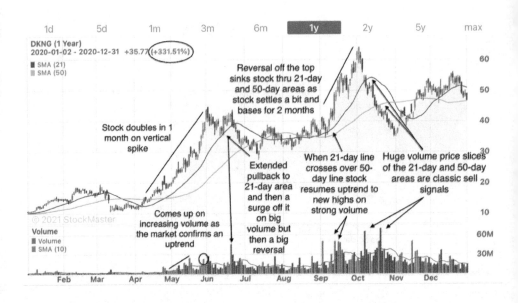

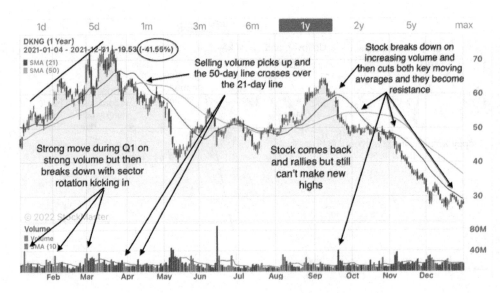

Figure 3-14 Draftkings, Inc. 2020 & 2021 Daily Chart. (StockMaster)

As you can see, the two years, though in uptrends for each year following the sharp sell-off in early 2020, played out in different ways. The following is from William J. O'Neil's book *How to Make Money in Stocks*, which I believe describes much of the markets in 2020 (first paragraph) and 2021 (second paragraph).

The really big money is usually made in the first one or two years of a normal new bull market cycle. It is during this period that you must always recognize, and fully capitalize upon, the golden opportunities presented.

The rest of the "up" cycle usually consists of back-and-forth movement in the market averages followed by a bear market. In the first or second year of a new bull market, there should be a few intermediate-term declines in the market averages. These usually last a couple of months, with the market indexes dropping by from 8% to an occasional 12% or 15%.

While 2020 was more of "buy the breakout and hold on until classic sell signals were fired off," the bulk of 2021 became more of a shorter swing trading environment that rewarded skittish trading as the year progressed. Richard D. Wyckoff and Gerald M. Loeb, two very successful stock traders from over 100 years ago who were active for many decades, both employed a skittish shorter-term strategy when the market called for it. Flexibility and the ability to adapt that flexibility into a strategy when the market calls for it is a key to success. Mark Minervini, who was profiled in the previous chapter and won the U.S. Investing Championship in 2021, reduced his time frames by taking advantage of quick shorter-term trades starting in Q1 because that's what the market was offering. He bought stocks setting up that met his criteria, then sold them quickly into short-term strength. He concentrated his positions heavily and nailed down short-term profits. And he always cuts his losses short when a trade goes against him. He repeated this strategy with high rates of turnover during the year and rotated into stocks the market kept offering as the best opportunities. He then compounded his returns month after month to break the performance record in the managed account stock division and capture the championship in the contest.

Mark proved that being flexible and nimble with a very tight risk-management strategy in 2021 was the key to strong returns because the market shifted from 2020. That shift in the market rewarded top traders who bought stocks on breakouts, rode them up just a bit, and then turned around and sold into that short-term strength. Breakouts seemed to work, but stocks had difficulty following up on those breakouts. That was not the case in 2020. In 2021, the top traders rotated into the next sector stocks that were offering those same opportunities and did the same thing. The longer the uptrend seemed to go on, the shorter the time frames for follow-throughs on breakouts got. That sector rotation in short time frames for breakouts is more conducive to a trader's market. In his book *Studies in Stock Speculation—Volume 1*, Richard D. Wyckoff describes the elements of a trader's market (and that was nearly 100 years ago). In summary, his advice for most traders is to stay out of trader's markets until a more definitive trend has been established, due to the more experienced reactionary quickness needed to take advantage of a trader's market environment. Employing that shorter-term strategy worked out very well in 2021 for some of the top traders covered in this book who had the experience to recognize what the market was doing and execute based on the opportunities it presented.

Also, Wyckoff conducted interviews with Jesse Livermore many decades ago that were reprinted by Windsor Books in 1984 in a booklet called *Jesse Livermore's Methods of Trading in Stocks.* The excerpt below relates to those times when uptrends get extended that don't experience any major corrections along the way but create choppy back-and-forth trading opportunities. Several of the top traders in 2021 related to what Livermore saw back in his day when the market started to experience this type of activity in early 2021, just before the shorter-term trading environment began.

As the market executes its series of intermediate swings and begins to approach the level when an important turning point is likely to occur, he looks for more frequent reactions, and, therefore, will very often liquidate all or part of his line on some of the strong bulges which occur in the upper stages of the market, or in what is known as the selling zone.

He is an active trader, for long ago he cured himself of jumping in and out of the market day after day. Next in importance to the trades which he makes are the intermediate swings running from ten to thirty points and from a week or two to a few months in duration. Let us say that the market is getting into the upper levels and, although not at the turning point, becomes overbought and the technical position is such that a reaction of ten to fifteen points is imminent. He decides that under such conditions it is best for him to reduce his line of long stocks in order that he may take advantage of whatever decline occurs by replacing them at lower prices. He may have twenty or thirty points profit in a certain lot of stock which he believes will sell at a higher figure eventually, but if he can close this out on the verge of a sharp reaction and replace it ten points cheaper, he has thereby reduced the original cost by that much.

What Livermore describes seems to relate closely to that early part of 2021 when big gains from 2020 were getting extended in many leading stocks. As the uptrend continued, we started to see sector rotation kick in by early spring 2021. As the year went along and the uptrend extended, sector rotation became much more common-place. That's when swing trading or scalping seemed to work best. And that's why Livermore adjusted his strategy during an aging uptrend because he knew more frequent reactions would occur as that uptrend kept creeping along. Applying that more active trad-ing strategy to the leading stocks as the 2021 uptrend moved along is what we learned from the top trader section in the prior chapter.

To adapt to changing uptrends as they age, one could tweak the strategy outlined in *Monster Stocks* (summarized earlier in this chap-ter) that has worked for decades and that worked so well in 2020. I would call this Maximum Monster Stock Strategy (MMSS). It should be noted that the steps outlined in *Monster Stocks* come from the meticulous and historical research of William J. O'Neil, Jesse Livermore, Richard D. Wyckoff, Gerald M. Loeb, Nicolas Darvas, and other successful growth and momentum traders from the past who studied how the best stocks acted before, during, and at the end of their successful runs. Each one then tweaked the system (added to it, adjusted it, etc.) to fit their own personality and style. They all discovered similarities in how great stocks became great percentage return stocks.

As discussed, when an uptrend continues on and matures, es-pecially after a year like 2020, the buying power typically begins to slow down. That typically happens if very few major corrections (of between 10% to 20% off index highs) and bear markets (indexes off 20% or more) occur during that uptrend. Also, there are several variations of market uptrends (and downtrends). There are strong uptrends, weaker uptrends, choppy uptrends, and so on. I use the H/L/G to get a sense of how strong an uptrend is by its net-trend numbers. Strong uptrends have very healthy numbers, and choppy uptrends have weaker, lower readings and can switch easily between positive and negative readings within days. You can view the index charts that relate to the net new high/new low numbers (H/L/G) for both 2020 (figure I-3) and 2021 (figure 2-33) to see those relationships.

Without a few corrections in the market during uptrends, buying power simply gets weaker as an advance ages due to most investors and traders being fully invested in strong uptrends. To combat that, one could tighten up the typical monster stock selling strategies. The classic monster stock growth selling strategies include sell signals when a big winner breaks the 21-day or the 50-day area, especially on larger volume. The other classic sell signal has been the climax run. Employing MMSS would consist of tightening that up a bit when the market environment changes. That would mean one could sell or trim positions in those stocks when the moving average for selling is moved up to the 10-day moving average area. Also, selling or trimming positions more often into strength before a climax run occurs is another tighter selling strategy. That type of selling calls for more frequent offensive "scaling out" sell transactions, instead of holding full positions until a classic break or climax run occurs. Selling then becomes more commonplace in choppy market environments. Additionally, not fully waiting for classic extensions off breakouts that reach 20% or 25% before one starts taking profits in a winning stock (a classic selling technique of *IBD*) is another offensive, tighter selling strategy. Doing that allows one to also buy back positions when rebounds off the 10-day and/or 21-day areas occur—similar to what Livermore mentioned above about getting back into the leaders as they started up again after a pullback. Adjusting those offensive and defensive selling strategies can be beneficial when the market calls for it. It's a more active approach than position trading but can reward those who want to stay active in aging uptrends. Instead of riding out those position trades in the strongest leading stocks through their pullbacks or rebasing stages, that MMSS strategy, if done correctly, could compound returns. All that means is one is reacting to what the market and leading stocks are doing as the market cycles through its stages. Staying in the zone and "the now" environment by tweaking strategies when it's called for can help one in future markets when conditions change.

The lessons mentioned at the beginning of this chapter will need to be repeated as the market cycles through its different stages and trends. As of the writing of this book, which is January 2022, the market had peaked in November 2021 and was correcting. During the month of January 2022, selling was dominating the market. There were many signals given just like there were in early 2020. Distribution days were piling up, leaders were topping, *IBD* downgraded to "market in correction," and the H/L/G was mostly negative. In fact, from mid-November until the end of January, 78% of the trading days were negative readings (40 of 51 trading days). That's a major trend change. Many top traders were in cash positions while some have traded the slim leadership that was providing opportunities in energy and just a few other select sectors. But for the time being, until the trend changes, which it always will at some point, protecting capital becomes a priority while keeping up the research work and keeping an eye on the market for future possible opportunities.

Conclusion

Observing something closely day after day gives one a keen eye to whatever is being observed. The stock market is both complex and contrary at the same time. But, as great traders discovered, observation, flexibility, and control (both in managing risk and your mindset) can go a long way in trying to stay on the profitable side of the market in a consistent manner over a period of time.

Those observation and flexibility skills defined differences in the markets in 2020 and 2021. Uptrends vary especially when they continue on for extended periods of time. Sticking to a solid and proven trading plan is critical. And that plan needs to fit the personality of each trader. But tweaking it based on the conditions of the market can be beneficial too. Just be sure not to constantly change from one type of strategy to another as the market moves. It's better to become an expert at one type of strategy versus a jack-of-all-trades. Subtle changes can be adjusted or added to your chosen strategy—the stock market is a never-ending learning process. Once your strategy works and your risk management control is tight, you need to be a strict disciplinarian. A disciplined approach is the key. Staying disciplined will keep you in your lane and, over time, will make you more consistent. Once you're consistent in your discipline and your approach, your results should start to consistently improve as well.

You can learn a lot about the stock market by having a basic understanding of how the best traders over many decades succeeded. You can learn a lot from their mistakes too. All the best traders studied the successful ones before them. But that foundational knowledge won't make you a successful trader. The path to success in the market is long and hard and often frustrating. But reading about and studying great traders is the start. Studying charts is also critical. Reducing tips and noise from other distractions is critical as well. Remember, everything ends up in price. Price reflects everyone's opinions, reactions, decisions, news, and so on. Observation is the other key. Find a proven strategy that fits you, learn from your mistakes, study the best traders and monster stocks from history, and stay disciplined in your approach.

Below I list some of the best stock market books ever written that have helped generations of traders. There have been thousands of books written on the stock market, but there are really only a handful worth studying. And that's not just my opinion. The books below are mentioned by many top traders as being the key foundational knowledge to their learning and understanding. Many are from decades ago and still stand as timeless classics. My own books used many of them as references. I read hundreds of market books, and though you will get something out of each one, the ones below offered the best education and foundations of knowledge on the market and trading.

Recommended works lists:

Top Market Books

How to Make Money in Stocks – William J. O'Neil – 1988

How I Made $2,000,000 in the Stock Market – Nicolas Darvas – 1960

How to Trade in Stocks – Jesse Livermore – 1940

The Battle for Investment Survival – Gerald M. Loeb – 1935

Studies in Tape Reading – Rollo Tape (aka Richard D. Wyckoff) – 1910

Trading in the Zone – Mark Douglas – 2000

Reminiscences of a Stock Operator – Edwin Lefevre – 1923

Tape Reading and Market Tactics – Humphrey Neill – 1931

Studies In Stock Speculation—Volume 1 – Richard D. Wyckoff – 1925

The Perfect Speculator – Brad Koteshwar – 2005

Trade like an O'Neil Disciple – Gil Morales and Chris Kacher – 2010

Think & Trade like a Champion – Mark Minervini – 2017

Trade like a Stock Market Wizard – Mark Minervini – 2013

Secrets for Profiting in Bull and Bear Markets – Stan Weinstein – 1988

You Can Still Make It in the Market – Nicolas Darvas – 1977

Stock Research and Apps:

Investor's Business Daily

StockMaster

TradingView

Bibliography

Boik, John. *Monster Stocks*. McGraw-Hill, 2008. All rights reserved.

Elder, Alexander, and Lovvorn, Kerry. *The New High – New Low Index*. SpikeTrade.com, 2012. All rights reserved.

Haller, Gilbert. *The Haller Theory of Stock Market Trends*. Gilbert Haller, 1965. All rights reserved.

O'Neil, William J. *How to Make Money in Stocks*. McGraw-Hill, 1988. All rights reserved.

Wyckoff, Richard D. *Studies in Stock Speculation – Volume 1*. Ticker Publishing Company, 1925. All rights reserved.

———. *Jesse Livermore's Methods of Trading in Stocks*. Windsor Books, 1984. All rights reserved.

About the Author

John Boik is the author of *Lessons from the Greatest Stock Traders of all Time*, which was chosen by *Barron's* as one of the top 25 books of 2004. He also wrote *How Legendary Traders Made Millions* and *Monster Stocks*, both endorsed by William J. O'Neil and *Investor's Business Daily*. You can follow John Boik on Twitter @monsterstocks1.

Acknowledgement

This book is dedicated to many of the pioneering growth stock traders who paved the way. Richard D. Wyckoff, Jesse Livermore, Bernard Baruch, Gerald M. Loeb, Jack Dreyfus, Nicolas Darvas, Peter Lynch, and William J. O'Neil among others. They set the course and passed on valuable knowledge to a new generation of traders.

A special thank you to several of todays successful traders for agreeing to be mentioned and profiled in this book. Jim Roppel, Eve Boboch, Oliver Kell, Matt Caruso, Ryan Pierpont, Roy Mattox, and especially Mark Minervini. Your results are inspiring and motivating to others.

I'd like to thank all of those at Elite Authors who helped put this together. It was a pleasure working with you. And thank you to all readers of this work, I hope it can assist you in reaching your investment and trading goals.

Made in the USA
Las Vegas, NV
28 July 2023

75330821R10085